my **revisi⏻n** notes

D1485274

AQA AS/A-level History

THE MAKING OF A SUPERPOWER: USA

1865–1975

Peter Clements

Series editor
David Ferriby

HODDER
EDUCATION
AN HACHETTE UK COMPANY

Acknowledgements

The Publishers would like to thank the following for permission to reproduce copyright material.

pp.17, 31 & 61 Excerpt(s) from *The Age of Reform* by Richard Hofstadter, copyright © 1955 by Richard Hofstadter. Used by permission of Alfred A. Knopf, an imprint of the Knopf Doubleday Publishing Group, a division of Penguin Random House LLC. All rights reserved; **pp.39 *A*, 55 & 63** *A History of the American People* by Paul Johnson. Published in 1997 by The Orion Publishing Group, London. Used with permission/*A History of the American People* by Paul Johnson. Used with permission of HarperCollins; **pp.50 & 93** Approximately four hundred and thirty-eight (438) words from *Colossus* by Niall Ferguson (Penguin Books, 2004, 2005). Copyright © Niall Ferguson, 2004/ *Colossus* by Niall Ferguson. Used with permission of Wylie Agency; **p.83 & 92** *Twentieth-Century America: A Brief History* by Thomas C. Reeves (2000): 2 extracts on pages 186 & 166–167 (as attachment submitted) totalling 409 words © 1999 by Oxford University Press, Inc. By Permission of Oxford University Press, USA.

Although every effort has been made to ensure that website addresses are correct at time of going to press, Hodder Education cannot be held responsible for the content of any website mentioned in this book. It is sometimes possible to find a relocated web page by typing in the address of the home page for a website in the URL window of your browser.

Hachette UK's policy is to use papers that are natural, renewable and recyclable products and made from wood grown in sustainable forests. The logging and manufacturing processes are expected to conform to the environmental regulations of the country of origin.

Orders: please contact Bookpoint Ltd, 130 Milton Park, Abingdon, Oxon OX14 4SE. Telephone: +44 (0)1235 827720. Fax: +44 (0)1235 400401. Email education@bookpoint. co.uk Lines are open from 9 a.m. to 5 p.m., Monday to Saturday, with a 24-hour message answering service. You can also order through our website: www.hoddereducation.co.uk

ISBN: 978 1 5104 1807 3

© Peter Clements 2018

First published in 2018 by
Hodder Education,
An Hachette UK Company
Carmelite House
50 Victoria Embankment
London EC4Y 0DZ

www.hoddereducation.co.uk

Impression number 10 9 8 7 6 5 4 3 2 1

Year   2022 2021 2020 2019 2018

Cover photo © Aleksandar Mijatovic – Fotolia

Illustrations by Integra

Typeset in Bembo Std Regular 11/13 Integra Software Services Pvt. Ltd., Pondicherry, India

Printed in Spain

A catalogue record for this title is available from the British Library.

My revision planner

REVISED

Part 2 Crises and the rise to world power, 1920–75

Introduction

Component 1: Breadth study

Component 1 involves the study of significant developments over an extended period of time (around 50 years at AS and 100 years at A-level) and an evaluation of historical interpretations.

The Making of a Superpower: USA, 1865–1975

The specification lists the content of The Making of a Superpower in two parts, each part being divided into two sections.
- Part 1 From Civil War to World War, 1865–1920:
  - The Era of Reconstruction and the Gilded Age, 1865–90
  - Populism, Progressivism and Imperialism, 1890–1920
- Part 2 Crises and the Rise to World Power, 1920–75 (A-level only):
  - Crisis of Identity, 1920–45 (A-level only)
  - The Superpower, 1945–75 (A-level only)

Although each period of study is set out in chronological sections in the specification, an exam question may arise from one or more of these sections.

The AS examination

The AS examination which you may be taking includes all the content in Part 1.

You are required to answer the following:
- Section A: one question on two contrasting interpretations: which is the more convincing? You need to identify the arguments in each extract and assess how convincing they are, using your knowledge, and then reach a judgement on which is the more convincing. The question is worth 25 marks.
- Section B: one essay question out of two. The questions will be set on a broad topic, reflecting that this is a breadth paper, and will require you to analyse whether you agree or disagree with a statement. Almost certainly, you will be doing both and reaching a balanced conclusion. The question is worth 25 marks.

The exam lasts one and a half hours, and you should spend about equal time on each section.

At AS, Component 1 will be worth a total of 50 marks and 50 per cent of the AS examination.

The A-level examination

The A-level examination at the end of the course includes all the content of both parts.

You are required to answer the following:
- Section A: one question on three interpretations: how convincing is each interpretation? You are *not* required to reach a conclusion about which might be the most convincing. You need to identify the arguments in each extract and use your knowledge to assess how convincing each one is. The question is worth 30 marks.
- Section B: two essay questions out of three. The questions will be set on a broad topic (usually covering 20–25 years). The question styles will vary but they will all require you to analyse factors and reach a conclusion. The focus may be on causation, or consequence, or continuity and change. Each question in this section is worth 25 marks.

The exam lasts for two and a half hours. You should spend about one hour on Section A and about 45 minutes on each of the two essays.

At A-level Component 1 will be worth a total of 80 marks and 40 per cent of the A-level.

In both the AS and A-level examinations you are being tested on the ability to:
- use relevant historical information (Sections A and B)
- evaluate different historical interpretations (Section A)
- the skill of analysing factors and reaching a judgement (Section B).

How to use this book

This book has been designed to help you develop the knowledge and skills necessary to succeed in the examination. The book is divided into four sections – one for each section of the A-level specification. Each section is made up of a series of topics organised into double-page spreads.

- On the left-hand page you will find a summary of the key content you will need to learn. Words in bold in the key content are defined in the Glossary (see pages 95–97).
- On the right-hand page you will find exam-focused activities.

Together these two strands of the book will provide you with the knowledge and skills essential for examination success.

▼ **Key historical content**

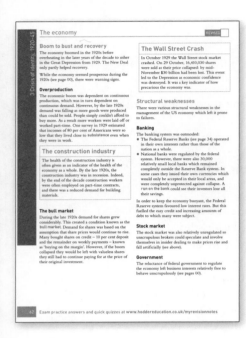

▼ **Exam-focused activities**

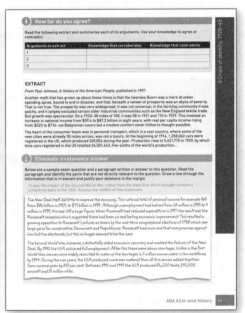

Examination activities

There are three levels of exam-focused activities:

- **Band 1** activities are designed to develop the foundation skills needed to pass the exam. These have a blue heading and this symbol:
- **Band 2** activities are designed to build on the skills developed in Band 1 activities and to help you to achieve a C grade. These have an orange heading and this symbol:
- **Band 3** activities are designed to enable you to access the highest grades. These have a purple heading and this symbol:

Some of the activities have answers or suggested answers on pages 102–104. These have the following symbol to indicate this:

Each section ends with an exam-style question and sample answers with examiner's commentary. This will give you guidance on what is expected to achieve the top grade.

You can also keep track of your revision by ticking off each topic heading in the book, or by ticking the checklist on the contents page. Tick each box when you have:

- revised and understood a topic
- completed the activities.

Quick quizzes at **www.hoddereducation.co.uk/myrevisionnotes**

Mark schemes

For some of the activities in the book it will be useful to refer to the mark schemes for this paper. Below are abbreviated forms.

Section A: Interpretations

Level	AS exam	A-level exam
1	Unsupported vague or general comments. Little understanding of the interpretations. (1–5)	Mostly general or vague comments. OR shows an accurate understanding of one extract only. (1–6)
2	Partial understanding of the interpretations. Undeveloped comments with a little knowledge. (6–10)	Some accurate comments on interpretations given in at least two of the extracts. Some analysis, but little evaluation. (7–12)
3	Reasonable understanding of interpretations. Some knowledge to support arguments. (11–15)	Some supported comments on the three interpretations with comments on strength, with some analysis and evaluation. (13–18)
4	Good understanding of interpretations. A supported conclusion, but not all comments well-substantiated and judgements may be limited. (16–20)	Good understanding of the interpretations, combined with knowledge of historical context, with mostly well-supported evaluation, but with minor limitations in depth and breadth. (19–24)
5	Good understanding of interpretations. Thorough evaluation of extracts leading to a well-substantiated judgement. (21–25)	Very good understanding of interpretations, combined with strong awareness of historical context to analyse and evaluate with well-supported arguments. (25–30)

Section B: Essays

Level	AS exam	A-level exam
1	Extremely limited or irrelevant information. Unsupported vague or generalist comments. (1–5)	Extremely limited or irrelevant information. Unsupported vague or generalist comments. (1–5)
2	Descriptive or partial, failing to grasp full demands of question. Limited in scope. (6–10)	Descriptive or partial, failing to grasp full demands of question. Limited in scope. (6–10)
3	Some understanding and answer is adequately organised. Information showing understanding of some key features. (11–15)	Understanding of question and a range of largely accurate information showing awareness of key issues and features, but lacking in precise detail. Some balance established. (11–15)
4	Understanding shown with range of largely accurate information showing awareness of some of key issues and features. (16–20)	Good understanding of question. Well-organised and effectively communicated with range of clear and specific supporting information showing good understanding of key features and issues, with some conceptual awareness. (16–20)
5	Good understanding. Well-organised and effectively communicated. Range of clear information showing good understanding and some conceptual awareness. (21–25)	Very good understanding of full demands of question. Well-organised and effectively delivered, with well-selected precise supporting information. Fully analytical with balanced argument and well-substantiated judgement. (21–25)

1 The era of Reconstruction and the gilded age, 1865–90

The American Civil War ended in April 1865 with the surrender of Southern forces. The war had cost 625,000 dead and more than $6 billion. After the assassination of **Republican** President Abraham Lincoln in April 1865, it was up to his successor, the **Democrat** Andrew Johnson to reconstruct and reunify the nation.

The weaknesses of federal government: Johnson, Grant and the failure of Radical Reconstruction

REVISED

The governance of the USA comprised the **president**, **Congress** and **Supreme Court**. There was a complex system of checks and balances to ensure no branch grew too powerful. However, this meant effective government was difficult in times of crisis when decisive actions were necessary. This is evident in the struggle over **Reconstruction** in the post-war period.

Johnson and the form of Reconstruction

Reconstruction involved two key issues:
- How far the Southern states should be punished for **seceding**.
- How African-Americans, mainly former slaves, should be treated in Southern states.

President Johnson wished to see the Southern states restored to the Union as soon as possible. He did not want to punish the South and felt each state should be responsible for how it treated its African-American population.

However, most members of Congress were Republicans who opposed this view. Many were **Radical Republicans** who wished to see harsh measures taken against the Southern states and legal measures taken to protect African-Americans. They gained more support as Southern states passed **Black Codes**, discriminating against African-Americans, and former **Confederate** politicians were restored to positions of influence.

Congressional victory over Johnson

Congress rejected Johnson's plans and passed a Civil Rights Act which overrode the Black Codes. Although Johnson **vetoed** this, Congress nevertheless ensured it came into law in April 1866. It was enshrined as the Fourteenth Amendment, giving all African-Americans born in the USA citizenship and full rights in law.

In the November 1866 **mid-term congressional elections**, Republicans gained a two-thirds majority in both Houses. Such was their disdain for Johnson that he was **impeached** over technical issues, and only survived by one vote. It came as no surprise that, in the 1868 election, he was easily defeated by a Republican former army general, Ulysses S. Grant.

Grant and the failure of Radical Reconstruction

Congress passed four separate Reconstruction Acts and placed the Southern states under military rule – but Reconstruction has mostly been seen as a failure:
- Many African-Americans were voted into political office, but were poorly educated and lacked the experience to govern effectively – although many regions saw the expansion of social services, improvements in education, developments of railroads and construction of levees to prevent flooding.
- The entry of **carpetbaggers** and **scalawags** into the political and economic spheres was deeply unpopular with Southern whites, because they were accused of exploitation and corruption.
- Many white people embarked on a policy of terror to intimidate African-Americans into withdrawing from the political process. Most notable was the **Ku Klux Klan** (KKK), formed in Tennessee in 1866.
- Another white group called **Redeemers** also attacked corruption in government. They found widespread support among the poorer classes.

By the late 1870s, many in the North were tired of the costs of Reconstruction. The result of the 1876 presidential election was contested. In the **Compromise of 1877** Southern Democrats agreed to support the Republican candidate Rutherford Hayes if federal troops were withdrawn, and Reconstruction ended. The Southern states became responsible again for their own governance.

Quick quizzes at **www.hoddereducation.co.uk/myrevisionnotes**

! Spot the mistake a

Below are a sample AS exam question and a paragraph written in answer to this question. Why does this paragraph not get high praise? What is wrong with the focus of the answer in this paragraph?

To what extent did problems with Reconstruction illustrate the weakness of federal government?

Reconstruction refers to the treatment of the defeated South after the Civil War. It involved two key issues: how far the Southern states should be punished and how African-Americans, mainly former slaves, should be treated in the Southern states. President Johnson was a Southerner himself: he wished to see the Southern states restored to the Union as quickly as possible. Johnson, moreover, was a Democrat, the party which gained most of its support in the South. However, many of the Northern Republicans wanted the South punished before it could be readmitted. They also wanted legal measures passed to protect African-Americans. Johnson found it difficult to impose his will because Congress was dominated by Republicans. The Southern Democrats of course were not there. The issue was made worse when Southern states began to pass Black Codes to limit opportunities for African-Americans.

! Delete as applicable

Below are a sample exam question and a paragraph written in answer to this question. Read the paragraph and decide which of the possible options (in bold) is most appropriate. Delete the least appropriate options and complete the paragraph by justifying your selection.

'The opposition of Southern whites was the most important reason for the failure of Reconstruction in the period 1865 to 1878.' How far do you agree to this statement in respect of why Reconstruction failed?

The opposition of Southern whites was the biggest reason for the failure of Reconstruction to a **great/fair/limited extent**. They resented Northern military occupation and the presence of scalawags and carpetbaggers who they felt were exploiting the process of Reconstruction for their own personal gain. Much racist feeling continued and the Ku Klux Klan and other groups created a campaign of terror and intimidation to ensure as many African-Americans as possible did not vote or participate in the political process. There were other reasons for its failure, however, such as the lack of experience and education which hampered many African-American legislators, however well-intentioned they were. Northerners too were getting tired of the cost and burden of Reconstruction. Therefore the opposition of whites was **slightly/to a certain extent/definitely** the main reason because

_____

_____

The politics of the Gilded Age, the era of weak presidents, and political corruption

The Gilded Age was the name broadly given to the final 30 years of the nineteenth century, as a time of weak government and widespread corruption.

The era of weak presidents

The period 1866 to 1896 saw a period dominated by congressional government where presidents tended to be weak and relatively ineffectual. Indeed real power lay with the Senate where members were often well established, and the relatively small membership (72 Senators in 1866) facilitated meaningful debate. The House of Representatives by contrast was generally seen as disorderly and indecisive. However, Democrats and Republicans agreed on many political issues.

Presidents, 1869–97

Name	Party	Year
U.S. Grant	Republican	1869
R. Hayes	Republican	1877
J. Garfield	Republican	1881
C. Arthur	Republican	1881
G. Cleveland	Democrat	1885
B. Harrison	Republican	1889
G. Cleveland	Democrat	1893

Civil service reform

Civil service reform became a long-standing issue during this period. As the role of federal government grew due to the increase in population and settlement of the continent (see page 20), its employees rose from 53,000 in 1871 to 256,000 by 1900. However, posts were largely filled by **patronage**. Politicians controlled specific appointments and gave them to people in return for political favours. This made for waste, inefficiency and corruption. Reformers called for the professionalisation of the bureaucracy with posts filled on merit.

It wasn't until 1883 that reform was finally successful. In 1881 President James Garfield had been assassinated by a disgruntled applicant for public office. This shocked many into supporting the professionalisation of the service. The Democrat Senator George Pendleton created the Pendleton Act to do this. The Act reserved 10 per cent of posts for appointments based on merit by competitive examination, and made it illegal for officeholders to make contributions to politicians. It would be extended as time went on, for example during the presidency of Democrat **Grover Cleveland**; he maintained the appointment of Republican officeholders if they were doing a good job and disdained to appoint people simply on the basis that they were Democrats.

Political corruption

Political corruption was widespread at all levels. Federal government was racked by a series of scandals:

- In September 1869 a group of speculators tried fraudulently to gain control of the gold market. President Grant was closely associated with two of their leaders, James Fisk and Jay Gould.
- Grant was personally honest but appointed corrupt cronies to high office. His private secretary, Orville E. Babcock, and Secretary of War, William W. Belknap, were involved in the Whiskey Ring scandal of 1875, which defrauded the taxpayer of millions in revenue.

City governments in particular were associated with corruption, with local political bosses controlling the votes of large groups through patronage and favours. The case of New York is typical. The so-called 'Tweed Ring' amassed millions of dollars before being broken up in 1873; one of its successor organisations, based in Tammany Hall and led by Richard Croker from the mid-1880s to 1900, effectively ran the city as a personal empire. Particularly important was control of the New York Customs House, where fraudulent practices led to millions being paid by importers and exporters in bribes.

Mugwumps

The Mugwumps were an influential group of Eastern Republicans who campaigned against corruption and sought more efficient government. They supported Democrat Grover Cleveland in the 1884 presidential election because of his reputation for efficiency as Governor of New York State; for example, he had sacrificed public support for political propriety when he vetoed a proposed fare reduction in public transport because the company did not have the legal right to do so.

Read the following extract and the two alternative answers to the question.

Which answer focuses more on the content and which one focuses more on the arguments of the interpretation? Explain your choice.

With reference to your understanding of the context, assess how convincing the arguments in this extract are in relation to the reasons why federal government was weak in the period 1865 to 1890.

Student 1

The extract states that presidents were weak and Congress dominated the government. The Senate overshadowed the House of Representatives. The Senate had been called a 'rich man's club' but it was capable of real debate. The House of Representatives in contrast was disorderly. I would say that the Senate was more effective than the House of Representatives but nevertheless there was little difference between the two political parties.

Student 2

The extract states that presidents were weak and Congress dominated the government. It goes on to argue, however, that although the Senate was accused of being a rich man's club, it was nevertheless capable of real debate. This suggests that the Senate might not necessarily be weak: indeed it had a good reputation in terms of qualities which might encourage effective governance, for example experience and intelligence. The extract asserts by contrast that the House of Representatives was disorderly. However, if there was little real disagreement between the political parties, the federal government, dominated by a strong Senate, could have operated effectively. Overall the extract suggests this may have been the case although it would need to give supporting evidence to back up the claim.

Extract A

From John Garraty, The American Nation *(Vol 2, 7th edition), published in 1991.*

A succession of weak presidents presided over the White House. Although the impeachment proceedings against Andrew Johnson had failed, Congress dominated the government. Within Congress, the Senate generally overshadowed the House of Representatives. In his novel *Democracy* (1880) the cynical Henry Adams wrote that the United States had 'a government of the people, by the people, for the benefit of Senators'. Critics called the Senate a 'rich man's club' and it did contain many millionaires. However, the true sources of the Senate's influence lay in the long tenure of many of its members (which enabled them to master the craft of politics), in the fact that it was small enough to encourage real debate and in its long-established relationship for wisdom, intelligence and statesmanship.

The House of Representatives, by contrast, was one of the most disorderly and inefficient legislative bodies in the world...

The great political parties professed undying enmity to each other, but they seldom took clearly opposing positions on the questions of the day. Democrats were separated from Republicans more by accidents of geography, religious affiliation, ethnic background and emotions than by economic issues.

Social, regional and ethnic divisions

Sectionalism, or the different developments within the different regions of the USA and the tensions between them, has been a significant factor in US history.

Divisions within and between North, South and West

The North

The North became increasingly industrial and urban (see pages 14 and 16). It was resented by many who lived elsewhere as dominating the shape of US political and economic development; it was felt that too many politicians represented Northern interests at the expense of others.

The New South

After the end of Reconstruction, people spoke of a **New South** which was modernising, and embracing new technologies. Railroads, for example, doubled in mileage during the 1880s, and made it possible to develop new industries such as coal mining in West Virginia. The city of Birmingham in Alabama with plentiful supplies of coal, iron and limestone nearby became the centre of a new steel industry. Entrepreneur James Buchanan revolutionised the tobacco industry through the use of machinery; each of his machines could produce 100,000 cigarettes per day.

However, despite these developments, most of the South remained agricultural and rural. The predominant crop was cotton. Most farmers worked as **sharecroppers**, allocated land and resources by the landowner in return for a percentage of the crop. If the value of crop failed to meet the debt, they would be in servitude to the landowner almost as much as a slave would.

The West

The development of the West was a major feature of US history – the movement of peoples to settle land and exploit natural resources while fighting off hostile Native Americans. Indeed the migration west was significant – for foreign-born migrants as much as those born in the USA. In the final quarter of the nineteenth century, one-third of the population of California and half that of Nevada and Arizona were foreign-born. Many in the West resented a distant federal government; they valued independence and 'rugged individualism'.

In the years following the Civil War, the development of the cattle industry had led to huge ranches feeding the growing populations of the Eastern cities, and gold, silver and copper discoveries had occasioned often short-lived hurried settlements such as within the Black Hills of Dakota in the late 1870s. However, most people moved west to farm, spurred on by the 1862 Homestead Act which allocated 160 acres free to those who could farm it for five years. Further Land Acts facilitated migration. However, comparatively few were able to make a comfortable living on 160 acres, and their difficulties in doing so were to lead to considerable tensions.

One issue of contention between the South and West on one hand and the North on the other was agriculture.

Farmers in the South and West

Farmers in the South and West faced huge problems of debt, often having to borrow to maintain their land, plant crops and look after their livestock. This borrowing was often on the expectations of harvesting and selling their produce at reasonable prices. However, markets could be unstable. If prices fell they could be ruined. These concerns led them to support ideas such as low interest rates and plentiful money, which were anathema in the more industrial and commercial North.

The position of African-Americans

African-Americans faced discrimination throughout the USA, but particularly so in the South. Here states increasingly passed '**Jim Crow**' laws to ensure segregation, and various methods were employed to prevent them from voting. These included unfair literacy tests and 'Grandfather clauses' which said that only those whose grandfathers had been able to vote could in fact vote in state elections – thus disqualifying descendants of former slaves. Meanwhile terror and intimidation continued with growing numbers of **lynchings**.

While many African-Americans began to move North at the beginning of the **Great Migration**, they were discouraged from doing so because Southern whites wanted to maintain their supply of cheap labour. Overall, however, they also faced discrimination in the North (see page 40).

! Mind map

Read the essay title below and complete the mind map to identify relevant reasons. Then prioritise your reasons by adding numbers to each oval box – with 1 as the most important reason and 6 as the least important.

How far were divisions between Northern, Southern and Western regions of the USA important in the period 1865 to 1890?

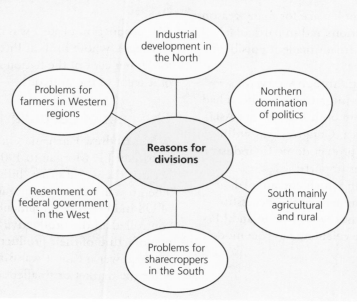

- Industrial development in the North
- Problems for farmers in Western regions
- Northern domination of politics
- **Reasons for divisions**
- Resentment of federal government in the West
- South mainly agricultural and rural
- Problems for sharecroppers in the South

! Support or challenge?

Below is a sample exam question which asks how far you agree with a specific statement. Below this is a series of general statements which are relevant to the question. Using your own knowledge and the information on the opposite page, decide whether these statements support or challenge the statement in the question.

'Tensions in US society in the period 1865 to 1890 are exemplified in the ways the West and South developed differently from the North.' How far do you agree with this statement?

	Support	Challenge
Farmers in the West and South faced burdens of debt.		
African-Americans in the South often worked as sharecroppers.		
African-Americans in the South often lived in positions of servitude.		
The New South was becoming more urban and industrial.		
The North was industrial and seemed to dominate politics.		
People in the West valued their independence and often resented federal government.		

Economic growth and the rise of corporations

The USA saw an industrial revolution in the years following the Civil War. From 1859 to 1899, the value of manufactured products rose by 622 per cent, from $1.8 billion to $13 billion.

Reasons for industrial expansion

Industrial development took place for many reasons:
- Improved communications and in particular the development of railroads made it possible to exploit natural resources.
- The USA was growing through westward expansion and massive migration – millions had moved to the USA from both Europe and Asia, and forcibly from Africa. Congress was willing to impose high tariffs to protect domestic industry by keeping out cheaper imports.
- There was an optimism which encouraged risk-taking and entrepreneurship – successful industrialists such as **Andrew Carnegie** and J.P. Morgan were far more celebrated as role models than politicians.

Railroads

Railroads saw huge growth in the years following the Civil War: 40,000 miles of track were laid between 1830 and 1870, and 110,000 miles in the following 20 years. The first transcontinental railway was completed in 1869; by 1900 there were five.

While the railroads were private companies, their growth was facilitated by massive land grants from federal government – up to 240,000 square miles which could then be sold off to settlers once the railway was complete. The railroads led to the introduction of common time zones across the USA in 1883, and were indirectly responsible for the development of a transcontinental telegraph system, whose stations followed the railroads.

Problems with railroads

Railroad owners could be corrupt, giving profitable contracts to construction companies they themselves owned, for example. With huge sums necessary for construction, railway finance was often unstable and, in the period of economic depression from 1873 to 1879, 25 per cent of US railroads failed.

Oil

The most successful oil firm was Standard Oil Company of Cleveland, founded by John D. Rockefeller in 1870. It embraced modern technologies and ruthless business practices to ensure that by 1879 it controlled 90 per cent of the oil-refining capacity of the USA. The industry grew with the introduction of the motor car in the early twentieth century.

Steel

The production of steel was dominated by Andrew Carnegie, whose mills at Pittsburgh were responsible for 70 per cent of the nation's output by 1890. Much of it went to the railroads.

The rise of corporations

When Andrew Carnegie sold his steel company to banker J.P. Morgan in 1901, United States Steel became the world's first 'billion-dollar corporation'. The growth of giant corporations had been a feature of US industrial development in which one company controlled all the productive processes in the manufacture of their product and the markets also. Their power meant it was difficult for newcomers to enter the market or smaller companies to remain.

Professionalisation of business

As big business developed it employed more managers, administrators and technical experts. The latter developed new processes and products. For example, Thomas Edison set up a research facility in 1876 at Menlo Park, New Jersey, which developed products such as phonographs and film projectors.

By 1900 half the working population of the USA were paid employees rather than self-employed.

Trusts and monopolies

Trusts were mergers and takeovers of smaller companies to create large corporations. By 1904, the largest 4 per cent of US companies were responsible for 57 per cent of total production. Examples are General Electricity, which controlled 85 per cent of the nation's output by the turn of the century, and Du Pont, which had a similar dominance in the chemical industry. Many of these large corporations were beginning to act like monopolies, which meant they could control supply and price, thus negating the idea of competition. Governments were often reluctant to tackle these corporations (see page 18).

ⓐ Summarise the arguments

Below are a sample exam question and one of the extracts referred to in the question. You must read the extract and identify the interpretation offered. Look for the arguments of the passage.

With reference to the extract and your contextual knowledge, how convincing do you find the extract in relation to the importance of railway development in the industrial development of the USA?

Interpretation offered by the extract:

_____

_____

EXTRACT

From J. Potter, 'Industrial America', in H.C. Allen and C.P. Hill (eds.), British Essays in American History, *published in 1969.*

The last factor in the transformation of the American scene was the completion in 1869 of the first trans-continental railroad, making the internal markets truly national in scope. Even more important than the immediate economic consequences of the first trans-continental was its symbolism. Optimism and buoyancy have never been lacking in American economic life. The challenge of the West was such that the conquest of space brought its own satisfaction; the act of reaching a place was as important as what was done on arrival. As one seemingly impossible physical barrier after another was broken down by human skill and ingenuity, the belief in human infallibility grew: no obstacles existed or could exist which could not be overcome in the course of time. 'The difficult can be done immediately; the impossible will take a little longer' became the slogan of American progress. The nation's success story thrived on success and the trans-continental railroad could be regarded as the greatest engineering achievement of all time.

ⓘ Simple essay style

Below is a sample A-level exam question. Use your own knowledge and the information on the opposite page to produce a plan for this question. Choose four general points, and provide three pieces of specific information to support each general point.

Once you have planned your essay, write the introduction and conclusion for the essay. The introduction should list the points to be discussed in the essay. The conclusion should summarise the key points and justify which point was the most important.

How accurate is it to say that the development of a national railroad network was the most important factor in the development of US industry in the period 1865 to 1890?

Developments in agriculture and the growth of urbanisation

The period 1865 to 1890 saw significant developments in agriculture and urbanisation.

Developments in agriculture

On the surface agriculture was thriving. The development of railroads saw the farming regions able to transport their produce to the growing urban areas of the North and beyond. Many of the problems of farming the Great Plains such as insufficient rainfall, relatively barren terrain and lack of timber for fencing had been overcome with technical developments such as wind-pumps to draw water from wells, the introduction of hardy strains of wheat and barbed wire for fencing. Between 1870 and 1900 the number of farms doubled to 5.7 million, and wheat production to 600 million bushels. The number of cattle trebled to 68 million. There were, however, significant problems in agriculture, some common throughout the sector and others specific to particular areas.

Debt

Many farmers were constantly in debt. Harvests and markets were unstable but generally farmers borrowed on expected income from the harvest. They often relied on middle men to sell their produce and had to pay steep railway charges to transport it. There was no central banking system: local banks charged high rates of interest – from 10 to 40 per cent. Many farmers lived on mortgaged property, and banks would often foreclose if they couldn't meet their payments. By 1900, as many as one-third of all farmers were tenants.

Sharecroppers

Sharecroppers (see page 12) were in an even worse position, especially in times of poor harvests.

The more affluent

Farmers in more settled areas, particularly in the North, tended to be more affluent because their families may have been long established in their farms and unburdened with a mortgage. Transport costs were lower because they were nearer to markets. Often in the South the more established farmers were those who accepted sharecroppers to whom they became creditors.

Agricultural protest

From the 1870s many farmers joined together in co-operatives, working together to try to eliminate the middle men and gain control of the purchase of goods and supplying markets. Interestingly, this **Granger movement** was most popular in Iowa and Illinois, two of the states most affected by debt and high interest rates. By 1890 these co-operatives had grown into the National Farmers' Alliance which would morph into the People's or Populist Party (see page 32).

The growth of urbanisation

The period saw considerable movement into cities primarily from people seeking work. The population of Chicago, a major railway hub and centre of the meat industry, grew from 30,000 to 1 million between 1850 and 1900. By this date the Union Stockyards covered over a square mile and supplied 80 per cent of the meat consumed in the USA. Meanwhile, the population of New York more than trebled from 1 million to 3.5 million between 1860 and 1900.

On the surface, cities showed the progress made in the USA. By the 1890s **skyscrapers** were being built with as many as 25 storeys. In 1902, 66 were being constructed in Lower Manhattan in New York alone. Undoubtedly, urbanisation benefited many, with employment opportunities (for example, in administration and business management) helping develop a new middle class. However, there were problems:

- Many lived in squalor and overcrowded conditions. For example, officials once found 150 lodgers sleeping on filthy floors in two buildings in New York.
- Political corruption was encouraged through the patronage system whereby people owed favours to local politicians (see page 10).

! Analysing an interpretation   a

Below is an extract to read. You are asked to summarise the interpretation about the problems facing farmers in the period 1865 to 1890 and then develop a counter-argument. Then use your knowledge to construct alternative arguments.

EXTRACT

From Richard Hofstadter, The Age of Reform, *published in 1968.*

From 1870 to 1900 more farm land was taken up than in all previous American history. By the mid-eighties a feverish land boom was under way... and it was the collapse of this boom that provides the immediate background of Western Populism. We may take the experience of Kansas as illustrative. The boom, originally based on the high prices of farm produce, had reached the point of artificial inflation by 1885. It had swept not only the country, where the rapid advance in prices had caused latecomers to buy and mortgage at hopelessly inflated values, but also the rising towns... As a state official later remarked, 'Most of us crossed the Mississippi or Missouri with no money but with a vast wealth of hope and courage... Haste to get rich has made us borrowers, and the borrower has made booms, and booms make men wild'... In the winter of 1887–88 this boom, which had been encouraged by railroads, newspapers and public officials, abruptly collapsed – in part because of drought in the western third of the state, in part because farm prices had stopped going up, and in part because the self-created confidence upon which the fever fed had broken.

! Eliminate irrelevance   a

Below are a sample A-level exam question and two paragraphs written in answer to this question. Read the paragraphs and identify the parts that are not directly relevant to the question. Draw a line through the information that is irrelevant and justify your deletions in the margin.

'The growth of urbanisation in the USA came at a significant human cost.' Assess the validity of this statement in respect of the growth of urbanisation in the USA in the period 1865 to 1890.

The period 1865 to 1890 saw considerable movement into cities primarily from people seeking work. As a result urbanisation grew – sometimes as a result of cities simply expanding into more rural areas. The population of Chicago, a major railway hub and centre of the meat industry, grew from 30,000 to 1 million between 1850 and 1900. By this date the Union Stockyards covered over a square mile and supplied 80 per cent of the meat consumed in the USA. Much of the meat came from the ranches of the West and was delivered by the growing railroad network – which created many jobs in both the meat and railroad industry and was another reason for the growth of Chicago. The population of New York meanwhile more than trebled from 1 million to 3.5 million between 1860 and 1900.

On the surface cities showed the progress made in the USA. By the 1890s skyscrapers were built with as many as 25 storeys. In 1902, 66 were being constructed in Lower Manhattan alone. Undoubtedly, urbanisation benefitted many, with employment opportunities, in administration and business management for example, helping develop a new middle class. However, there were significant problems. Many lived in squalor and overcrowded conditions; for example, officials found 150 lodgers sleeping on filthy floors in two buildings in New York. Political corruption moreover was encouraged through the patronage system whereby people owed favours to local politicians.

Laissez-faire dominance and its consequences

Governments during the period 1865 to 1890 tended to practise a policy of *laissez-faire*, particularly in relation to the economy and social issues. This suggested they did not get involved in people's lives. The vast majority of people would be most likely to come across federal government officials only through the officials who delivered their mail. Most provisions such as social services and education were the responsibility of individual states and were highly variable. Federal government did little except conduct foreign affairs and diplomacy; for example, there was no federal legislation against child labour.

Congressional government

We have seen that this was a period of weak presidents (see page 10). President Hayes believed that Congress should be responsible for solving the nation's problems, not the president. For example, he was concerned about the treatment of African-Americans in the South and supported civil service reform – but having shared his concerns with Congress, he largely felt his role was done. He did not initiate any relevant legislation. Similarly President Arthur urged Congress to reduce tariffs but did little to press the issue.

Having said this, however, federal governments did act from time to time, often at the instigation of Congress. In President Harrison's time in office from 1889 to 1893, for example, it spent $1 billion on legislation such as:

- Raising tariffs to an all-time high, particularly with the McKinley tariff of 1890. This increased tariffs on imported manufactured goods by almost 50 per cent while making imports such as sugar and coffee tax-free. It therefore protected the interests of US manufacturers and US agricultural interests abroad while making manufactured goods more expensive for US consumers.
- Passing anti-trust measures (see below).
- Committing the government to buying, through the Silver Purchase Act of 1890, 4.5 million ounces of silver each month to produce more money in circulation.

These measures may have been in response to pressure from specific groups but showed *laissez-faire* was not all embracing.

Congressional support for the wealthy

Congress seemed primarily to support industrial and wealthy interests. For example, it had few qualms about imposing high tariffs to protect industry, but had quickly abolished the graduated income tax introduced during the Civil War. When this was briefly reintroduced in 1894, it was abandoned the following year with barely a debate. The system was much criticised, notably by a British political scientist, James Bryce, who argued that Congress was oblivious of new developments in society which were changing the USA, such as the growth of urbanisation and its attendant social problems or agricultural concerns.

Legislation

Congress responded to the deep unpopularity of trusts. Public antipathy was so great that one jury acquitted the kidnapper of a son of a prominent member of the Beef Trust, while influential writers such as Henry George were exposing plentiful examples of unfair practices and corruption.

Interstate Commerce Act, 1887

This Act said all railroad charges should be fair and set up an Interstate Commerce Commission to supervise them. Railroads were made to publish their rates; they had been overcharging smaller-scale firms and offering rebates to larger ones. While the government wasn't empowered to set rates, it did set an important break with *laissez-faire* in its supervisory role.

Sherman Anti-Trust Act, 1890

Any trust that restricted trade between states or the USA and foreign nations was declared illegal. While this seemed impressive, its terms were deliberately vague, and in 1895 it was weakened by a hostile Supreme Court ruling. The Court judged that the American Sugar Company had not violated the law by taking over a number of competitors: even though the company controlled 98 per cent of all sugar refining in the USA, the Court held that it did not disrupt trade in that industry.

Spot the mistake

Below are a sample exam question and a paragraph written in answer to this question. Why does this paragraph not get high praise? What is wrong with the focus of the answer in this paragraph?

'During the period 1865 to 1890, federal governments only represented the interests of the wealthy and big business.' How far do you agree with this statement?

During the period 1865 to 1890 federal government only represented the interests of the wealthy and big business. It did not, for example, pass any legislation to regulate child labour or improve the shocking living conditions in big cities. It could have passed slum clearance measures or built sewers as in Britain. President Hayes didn't even think it was the job of the president to pass legislation. No wonder Congress spent its time passing high tariffs in the interests of big business. Having said this, it did pass some anti-trust measures such as the 1890 Sherman Anti-Trust Act. However, these were often vaguely worded and not very effective.

Spectrum of importance

Below are a sample exam question and a list of general points which could be used to answer the question. Use your own knowledge and the information on the opposite page to reach a judgement about the importance of these general points to the question posed. Write numbers on the spectrum below to indicate their relative importance. Having done this, write a brief justification of your placement, explaining why some of these factors are more important than others. The resulting diagram could form the basis of an essay plan.

To what extent did federal governments pursue *laissez-faire* policies during the period 1865 to 1890?

1   Legislation to regulate trusts, e.g. Interstate Commerce Act, 1885, and Sherman Anti-Trust Act, 1890

2   High tariffs

3   Little social reform

4   Belief by President Hayes that Congress rather than the president was responsible for initiating legislation

5   Silver Purchase Act, 1890

Least important ←——————————————————————————————→ Most important

The impact of the ending of the frontier

The closing of the frontier

Western expansion and the settlement of the frontier had long held a significant resonance in the USA. In the early 1890s two developments suggested the western frontier was now closed.

The 1890 US Census Bureau declaration

In 1890 the US Census Bureau declared that now the West was fully settled there was no longer a frontier. For the first time there was no undeveloped land available in the United States.

The 1893 Turner thesis

F.W. Turner was an academic historian whose 1893 conference paper, '*The Significance of the Frontier in American History*', had a wide influence both at the time and has been much debated ever since. Turner argued that the idea of the frontier had been deeply significant in the development of the USA:

- The availability of free land acted as a safety valve against social disharmony.
- The difficulty of settlement led to self-reliance and independence among Americans.

It followed then that the closing of the frontier would have deep significance.

The significance of the ending of the frontier

Clearly both the Census Bureau and Turner were overstating the case. There was much land within the USA which was still unoccupied and vast resources still to be developed. Life on the frontier had been so harsh that many settlers had returned East. The nature of its settlement had changed over time and within different regions.

The cattle empire

Vast cattle ranches had developed in the years following the Civil War based on the open range in which cattle roamed over huge unfenced areas before being driven to **railheads** by cowboys on **long drives**. However, the extension of railroads made long drives less necessary while particularly harsh winters in 1885 and 1887 killed as many as 90 per cent of the cattle. Although the industry recovered by importing new breeds, they needed more care, and ranches became smaller, enclosed often by barbed wire.

Farming

The Great Plains became largely an area of farms growing wheat and other crops using machinery such as reapers and threshing machines. Some large-scale farms that were able to afford new technologies and methods were appearing.

The myth of the frontier

Despite the reality of settlement, the myth of the frontier was that the USA always needed new areas to settle and civilise, that Americans were a restless people always seeking a new challenge, and it was this restlessness and drive that made them dynamic. This myth has resonated deeply in American history.

The myth of the frontier was perpetuated in popular entertainment about the West with 'Wild West' shows and rodeos showing cowboy riding and roping skills, novels and, later, films which celebrated wars against Native Americans and the fight against lawlessness – in other words, bringing 'civilisation' to a wild area.

However, on a deeper level, the closing of the western frontier led to the issue of the opening of new ones: it coincided with the growth of ideas of imperialism within the USA (see page 42). If internal frontiers no longer existed, then external ones did – in the form of partially and undeveloped countries, many within the American continent. Americans turned to look for these new frontiers.

Comparing interpretations

With reference to the two extracts and your understanding of the historical context, which do you find more convincing in explaining the importance of the frontier in American history?

Compare the arguments in the two extracts, and use your contextual knowledge to decide which is more convincing. You could shade the sections of each extract that you agree with.

Then set out the plan of your answer identifying agreements between the two extracts, and then disagreements, using your contextual knowledge.

Extract A argument(s)	Extract B argument(s)	Your contextual knowledge
Agreements	Agreements	
Disagreements	Disagreements	

EXTRACT 1

From Roger Thompson, The Golden Door: A History of the United States 1607 to 1945, *published in 1969.*

His [Turner's] thesis is contained in the opening paragraph of his essay: 'American history has been in a large degree the history of the colonisation of the Great West. The existence of an area of free land, its continuous recession and the advance of American settlement westward explain American development' ... He defined the frontier as 'the line of most rapid and effective Americanisation'. According to Turner, the presence of the great western opportunity had encouraged the rise of democracy and of rugged individualism, the fostering of national rather than local or sectional loyalties, American drive and resourcefulness and the national belief in egalitarianism...

To Turner, the whole of American history since Jamestown [the first recorded settlement] was a series of waves, lapping ever further westward to new high-water marks. Accepting differences imposed by time and place, he nonetheless emphasised the similarity in the stages of settlement of each new frontier zone: hunter, trader, miner or grazer or pioneer, farmer, capitalist. As each new area of western land rose to maturity, as each new belt of states was admitted to the Union, frontier policies and beliefs were forced on the more conservative elements of the nation.

EXTRACT 2

From David Reynolds, America, Empire of Liberty, *published in 2009.*

The 'frontier' is still a feature of American scholarship, but understood very differently from Turner's days. The concern for minorities that fostered 'black studies' also encouraged a new interest in Indian history – the other side of the frontier divide. The Europeans had not stumbled on 'virgin land': as numerous legal cases have now acknowledged, they often seized the land from the original inhabitants through acts of territorial rape. In some accounts the Native Americans emerge as simple 'victims' of progressive American expansion. More subtly the frontier has been redefined not as a crude line of white settler advance into a barren wilderness but as a shifting zone of interaction between different cultures, a 'middle ground'. That interaction involved conflict but also accommodation as distinctive social patterns emerged from the process of mixing, sharing and even intermarriage.

The limits of foreign engagement and continuation of isolationism

In the nineteenth century the USA seemed detached from foreign entanglements. This policy is usually referred to as **isolationism**.

The USA was able to avoid entanglement in foreign issues for a variety of reasons:

- The geographical position of the USA, far away from the great powers of Europe, meant it could avoid involvement in international issues.
- The USA felt itself unique in that it had been set up as a new republic, born out of rebellion against Britain, an **imperial power**: it had no desire to get involved with powers whose values it rejected.
- It had been populated often by people seeking to escape persecution in their own lands, who wanted to make a new start, not become involved in the affairs of the countries they had left.

The continuation of the Monroe Doctrine

In 1823 President James Monroe issued his doctrine, warning European powers against involvement in affairs on the American continent. At the time this was largely because countries in Latin and South America were fighting for independence from Spain. However, the Monroe Doctrine was applied against French involvement in Mexico in 1866.

French involvement in Mexico

While the USA was preoccupied with its Civil War, the French had established a puppet emperor, Maximilian, in Mexico supported by French troops. This led to a rebellion by Mexican forces. Once the Civil War was over, US **Secretary of State William H. Seward** demanded the French withdraw and moved 5,000 troops to the Mexican border. The French acceded to Seward's demands and withdrew, leaving Maximilian to his fate.

However, the Monroe Doctrine was not applied consistently. The USA did not prevent Britain from acquiring the colonies of British Guiana and Honduras in 1831 and 1832 respectively, and the Spanish maintained their control of Cuba until the end of the century (see page 42).

How far isolationism was pursued

In reality the USA had never strictly followed a policy of isolationism. It simply had too many interests. It had, for example, gone to war with Mexico in the 1840s to acquire vast stretches of territory north of the Rio Grande, which were to become the states of California, Arizona and New Mexico.

- William Seward (Secretary of State 1861–68) pursued expansionist policies such as the purchase of Alaska from Russia in 1867 (see page 24).
- Seward acquired the uninhabited Midway islands in the Pacific Ocean in 1867, originally to obtain supplies of guano for use in the manufacture of gunpowder and fertiliser.
- Congress blocked an attempt in 1870 to acquire the Dominican Republic because it saw no advantage from annexation.
- In 1884 Republican leader James Blaine advocated closer links with Latin America, especially for trade.
- In 1898 the USA acquired its first major Pacific naval base in Pearl Harbor on the island of Hawaii.

Britain

The USA had various disagreements with Britain, noticeably over:

- the location of borders between Oregon territory and Canada, a British colony
- the perceived British support for the Confederacy during the Civil War. Indeed Britain was blamed for supplying the South with cruisers which sank 100,000 tons of Northern shipping. Only in 1871 was this dispute finally solved, with Britain agreeing to pay $15.5 million compensation.

East Asia

The USA was quick to recognise the potential of East Asia for trade, particularly after ports on the western seaboard such as San Francisco were developed in the 1840s; a treaty with China in 1844 and Japan in 1857 opened up their markets. Indeed the Burlingame treaty of 1868 endorsed free trade and free movement of people between the USA and China, in part to stimulate Chinese immigration for work on railway building in the USA; this was negated by the Chinese Exclusion Act of 1882 when legislators feared Chinese immigration was too high.

RAG – rate the timeline a

Below are a sample exam question and a timeline. Read the question, study the timeline and, using three coloured pens, put a Red, Amber or Green star next to the events to show the following:

- ● Red: Events and policies that have no relevance to the question.
- ● Amber: Events and policies that have some significance to the question.
- ● Green: Events and policies that are directly relevant to the question.

To what extent was the policy of isolationism pursued in the years 1865 to 1890?

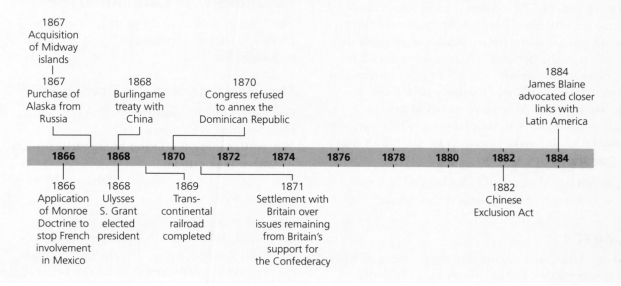

 Simple essay style

Below is a sample exam question. Use your own knowledge and the information on the opposite page to produce a plan for this question. Choose four general points, and provide three pieces of specific information to support each general point.

Once you have planned your essay, write the introduction and conclusion for the essay. The introduction should list the points to be discussed in the essay. The conclusion should summarise the key points and justify which point was the most important.

How accurate is it to say that the wealth and influence of the USA were the main reasons for its inability to pursue policies of isolationism during the period 1865 to 1890?

Territorial consolidation and tensions over Canada

The period 1865 to 1890 saw the USA consolidate its territory on the American continent and take an increasing interest in Latin America.

Consolidation of territory: Alaska

In 1867, the USA purchased Alaska from Russia for the sum of $7.2 million – mainly to remove the presence of Russia from the American continent. Many people at the time couldn't understand the motives or the benefits – Alaska was referred to as (Secretary of State) 'Seward's Folly'. However, Seward had an ulterior motive – he felt the development of Alaskan ports might provide a gateway to northern Asia, where US merchant ships could fuel and make provision for the long voyage across the Pacific Ocean.

If necessary Alaska could also be used as a useful base in the event of disputes with Canada.

Canada

Many Americans did not like the presence of what was effectively a British colony on their doorstep. Many Canadians feared their country would be vulnerable to an attack from the USA in the event of disputes with Britain. As a result relations between the two countries were often tense during the nineteenth century, but particularly so in the years following the Civil War when the issue of Canada got caught up in the compensation claims relating to British support for the Confederacy (see page 22).

After Seward bought Alaska, he half-expected the neighbouring Canadian province of British Columbia to request annexation. However, others felt that this province, plus Nova Scotia and Manitoba, should be annexed by the USA in lieu of compensation from Britain. This didn't happen, in part because there was no great support within the USA preoccupied with Reconstruction – and even less support in the Canadian provinces.

Clearly there were close relations too with Canada, not least in Canadian migration southwards in the 1870s and 1880s when the USA seemed to be developing at a much faster rate. Nonetheless, tensions remained, not least because of the raids on Canadian territory by supporters of Irish independence using the USA as a base. However, most disputes, for example over fishing rights, were settled by arbitration.

Relations with Latin America

The USA hoped to develop its influence in Latin America in terms of political influence and trading links.

First Pan-American Conference, 1889

Delegates from 18 countries met in Washington in October 1889 with two goals:
1 A customs union offering free trade across the American continent.
2 A system for international arbitration to avoid future wars.

However, these goals seemed too ambitious, particularly when the USA was preparing the McKinley tariff (see page 18), the highest in its history, and Latin American delegates believed the USA would use any arbitration system to dominate the continent. As a result, little was agreed beyond some trade agreements and a weak arbitration system, which was signed by only half the delegates. Nevertheless, the precedent was set for future agreements and co-operation.

By the late 1880s, moreover, more Americans were supporting foreign involvement with the closure of the western frontier and the development of the economy. Some indeed felt the USA might be ready for imperial expansion (see page 42).

Protection of trade

The growth of trade required military protection from army and naval forces. However, by the 1880s the army was limited to 25,000 men, and the USA had only the twelfth largest military in the world. Successive Naval Secretaries called for expansion of the service but their efforts were rebuffed until the following decade.

How far do you agree?

Read the extract below and summarise each of its arguments. Use your knowledge to agree or contradict.

Arguments in extract	Knowledge that agrees	Knowledge that contradicts
1		
2		
3		

EXTRACT

From Carl N. Degler, Out of Our Past, *published in 1984.*

William Seward's acquisition of Alaska and the Midway islands in 1867 was [also] dictated by a belief, as he said, that 'the Pacific Ocean, its shores, its islands and the vast regions beyond will become the chief theatre of events in the world's thereafter'.

Neither the acquisition of a Pacific frontage nor Alaska, however, moved the United States of the immediate post-Civil War years into extra-continental expansion. Indeed, even Seward's acquisition of Alaska was ridiculed as the purchase of a useless icebox. Grant's interest in extending Americans suzerainty [control] over Santo Domingo in 1870 was killed off by a resolute Senate and public, which firmly rejected expansion outside of established continental boundaries. In short, neither the prophesies of a secretary of state nor the activism of an imperial-minded president could move Americans to colonial acquisition. But what officials could not achieve in 1870, other less personal forces would do in the 1890s.

Recommended reading

- C. Calhoun (ed.), *The Gilded Age* (2007)
- John Garraty, *The American Nation*, 7th edition (1991), pages 448–536
- Richard Hofstadter, *The Age of Reform* (1968)
- Roger Thompson, *The Golden Door: A History of the United States 1607–1945* (1969), Chapters 6 and 7

Exam focus (AS)

Below is a sample Level 5 AS essay. Read it and the comments around it.

'The USA was too influential to be consistently able to pursue isolationist policies during the period 1865 to 1890.' Explain why you agree or disagree with this view.

Many Americans in the period 1865 to 1890 continued to support a detachment from foreign entanglements. However, this does not necessarily imply isolationism or remaining aloof as far as possible from foreign entanglements. In reality the USA was too powerful and too influential ever to pursue strict policies of isolationism, although its detachment could suggest otherwise. Foreign policy in the period 1865 to 1890 was in fact a mixture of detachment and involvement, although the interventionist impulse became much more marked in the following decade.

Engagement with essay and discussion of key term.

Introductory judgement.

The USA was able to avoid entanglement in foreign issues for a variety of reasons: the geographical position of the USA, distant from the great powers of Europe, meant it could avoid involvement in international issues. It had, moreover, no wish to become involved with European powers: many of its population had migrated to the USA to avoid European tensions: there simply was no will either at popular or government level to become embroiled in them. This was to an extent shown in the inconsistent application of the Monroe Doctrine of 1823, which warned European powers away from involvement in the affairs of countries of the American continent. It had, for example, done nothing to prevent British encroachment in Honduras in 1832, but had warned off the French from their entanglement in Mexico in the 1860s; indeed William H. Seward had moved 5000 troops to the border in 1866.

Clear paragraph introduction.

Well-structured factors.

Seward, Secretary of State from 1861 to 1868, was in fact an interventionist who believed the USA had a significant role to play in international affairs, as well as being the dominant force on the American continent. He sought to extend the influence of the USA. He purchased Alaska from Russia in 1867 for the sum of $7.2 million, for example – mainly to remove the presence of Russia from the continent. Many people at the time couldn't understand the motives. However, Seward had an ulterior purpose – he felt the development of Alaskan ports might provide a gateway to northern Asia, where US merchant ships could fuel and make provision for the long voyage across the Pacific Ocean. Alaska could also, if necessary, be used as a useful base in the event of disputes with Canada. Seward also acquired the uninhabited Midway islands in the Pacific Ocean in 1867, originally to obtain supplies of guano for use in the manufacture of gunpowder and fertiliser, but also for their potential as a staging post for vessels en route to markets in Asia.

Shows influence of Seward as Secretary of State.

However, after Seward, Congress in particular became more assertive in promoting non-involvement. In 1870, for example, it blocked an attempt to acquire the Dominican Republic because it saw no advantage from annexation. In 1871 tensions with Britain over its perceived support for the Confederacy in the Civil War were resolved by $15.5 million compensation. The Burlingame Treaty of 1868 had facilitated trade with China and stimulated Chinese migration, but the 1882 Chinese Exclusion Act stopped the latter. Calls for a stronger navy to protect US trading interests, for example in the Far East, were rejected by Congress – although in 1887 the USA was granted the right to build a naval base at Pearl Harbor in Hawaii.

Strikes a balance in terms of the question.

While many supported this detachment, others were becoming more interventionist, recognising the potential influence of the United States on the world stage. They saw the benefits particularly of trading links. In 1884, for example, Republican leader James Blaine advocated closer links with Latin America especially for trade. However, efforts to draw closer were first met with distrust from Latin American countries about US motives. The first Pan-American Conference in 1889 met with

Explains trends.

little success. It had two ambitious goals: a customs union offering free trade across the American continent and a system for international arbitration to avoid future wars. However, in the face of the high McKinley tariff in 1890 and fears about US power and influence, its agreements were weak, vague and only signed by half the 18 delegates. Nevertheless a precedent was set for future involvements. Many Latin American countries feared the USA would be too influential in the region. — Explains importance.

The period 1865 to 1890 saw greater involvement in foreign affairs, particularly during the period of office of William H. Seward, but after his departure, the policy veered towards greater isolationism. However, overall the trend was clearly for greater involvement and the seeds of the more expansionist foreign policy of the 1890s were set during this period, for example in the acquisition of more territory, and beginnings of formal agreements with Latin America. The USA was too influential to be consistently able to pursue isolationist policies during the period 1865 to 1890. — Tightly argued conclusion with valid judgement based on the question focus and the content of the essay.

This is well argued and structured, with question focus maintained throughout. There is a range of information to support the points being made. This essay should reach Level 5.

Reverse engineering

The best essays are based on careful plans. Read the essay and the examiner's comments and try to work out the general points of the plan used to write the essay. Once you have done this, note down the specific examples used to support each general point.

Exam focus (A-level)

Below is a sample Level 5 essay. It was written in response to an A-level question. Read it and the comments around it.

'*Laissez-faire* policies from weak governments boosted the interests of big business in the USA in the period 1868 to 1890.' How far do you agree with this statement?

The period of 1868 to 1890 saw a succession of weak presidents and indeed the period has been called one of congressional government. However, this does not in itself imply weak government. It was the policies such as *laissez-faire* or getting involved as little as possible in the economy which may have facilitated the interests of big business. Overall, governments may have acted in their interests, although the evidence is not entirely consistent and there may have been the beginnings of a reversal particularly in the later period covered by the question.

> **Immediate engagement with the question.**

> **Meaning of *laissez-faire* is understood.**

> **Introductory judgement.**

The USA made huge developments in industry in the years following the Civil War. Between 1859 and 1899, the value of manufactured products rose by 622 per cent, from $1.8 billion to $13 billion. Much of this was achieved by big business, exemplified by large corporations often founded by dynamic entrepreneurs, such as Cornelius Vanderbilt in railroads and Andrew Carnegie in steel production. While factors such as the development of the railroads facilitated industrial growth, it was undoubtedly also helped by the reluctance of federal government to regulate industrial practices. Governments tended to practise a policy of *laissez-faire*, particularly in relation to the economy and social issues. This suggested they did not get involved in people's lives; for example, there was no legislation on such issues as child labour or employment practices. The Republican presidents in particular did not seek an active role. President Hayes believed that Congress should be responsible for solving the nation's problems not the president. For example, he was concerned about the treatment of African-Americans in the South and supported civil service reform – but having shared his concerns with Congress, he largely felt his role was done. He did not initiate any relevant legislation. Similarly President Arthur urged Congress to reduce tariffs but did little to press the issue. However, the only Democratic president of the period, Grover Cleveland, was sometimes more proactive, supporting the Interstate Commerce Act discussed below and in 1887 removing land grants from railroad companies. Federal governments did, however, introduce troops to break strikes as in the National Railroad Strike of 1877 where 25 strikers were shot. This was justified in terms of public order but it also helped big business impose their will on their workforce in order to reduce labour costs and maximise their profits .

> **Shows context of question.**

> **Example a little off question focus.**

> **Examples to strike a balance.**

Nevertheless federal governments did act from time to time, often at the instigation of Congress but breaking with the idea of *laissez-faire*. Some measures favoured big business and others did not. For example, it raised tariffs to an all-time high, particularly with the McKinley tariff of 1890. This increased tariffs on imported manufactured goods by almost 50 per cent while making imports such as sugar and coffee free. It therefore protected the interests of US manufacturers and US agricultural interests abroad while making manufactured goods more expensive for US consumers. However, supporters argued high tariffs favoured workers by guaranteeing jobs as well as business interests.

> **Balance maintained.**

On the other hand Congress passed anti-trust measures such as the 1885 Interstate Commerce Act. This insisted all railway charges should be fair, and it set up an Interstate Commerce Commission to supervise them. Railroads were made to publish their rates; they had been overcharging smaller-scale firms and offering rebates to larger ones. However, its effect was limited by the fact that the government wasn't empowered to set rates. Similarly, the Sherman Anti-Trust Act 1890 declared that any trust that restricted trade between states or the USA and foreign nations was illegal. While this may have seemed impressive, its terms were deliberately vague, and in 1895 it was weakened by

Quick quizzes at **www.hoddereducation.co.uk/myrevisionnotes**

a hostile Supreme Court ruling. The court judged that the American Sugar Company had not violated the law by taking over a number of competitors: even though the company controlled 98 per cent of all sugar refining in the USA, the court held that it did not disrupt trade in that industry.

Lots of relevant knowledge in support.

These measures may have enjoyed only a limited effect but they did set an important break with *laissez-faire* in their supervisory role and showed that governments would act where necessary. The Silver Purchase Act in 1890 committed the government to buying 4.5 million ounces of silver each month to produce more money in circulation. This was an increasing issue for Western and Southern interests and was to feature heavily both in the Populist movement and 1896 presidential election.

Could be made more relevant.

The period 1868 to 1890 saw so-called congressional government and *laissez-faire* as a dominant policy. Undoubtedly, non-involvement in the economy favoured business interests as they could conduct their affairs without regulation. Where government did get involved, for example in imposing high tariffs, this reflected their interests. However, there were also the beginnings of anti-trust legislation and regulation, for example of the railroads. These may not have been hugely effective but did set precedents for the future. The picture therefore is more complex than a simple assertion about *laissez-faire* would suggest. While it was broadly still true that weak government and *laissez-faire* facilitated big business interests, changes were gradually being introduced.

Well-structured conclusion with valid judgement in terms of question.

This is a very good essay. It addresses the issues well with valid examples and comes to a nuanced conclusion with a focused judgement. However, it also meanders at times from the question with its examples and the penultimate paragraph could be made more relevant. Despite this the argument, analysis and use of valid example, with a focused introduction and conclusion, should ensure it attains Level 5.

The eyes of an examiner

It would be useful to look at this answer 'through the eyes' of the examiner. The examiner will look for a range of explanation. In the margin, therefore, write a word or phrase which sums up each specific explanation as it appears. Good answers present at least three explanations and discuss each one in a separate paragraph. Also, highlight or underline where any attempts are made to show links between explanations or where prioritisation occurs.

2 Populism, progressivism and imperialism, 1890–1920

Political tensions and divisions

The period 1890 to 1920 saw political tensions as exemplified by the rise of the Populist movement and **progressivism**. This resulted in large part from:
- a reaction to the power and influence of big business
- the perceived dominance of the industrial North in promoting political policies in their own interests at the expense of other sectors.

The reaction against big business at national and state level

One increasing concern was that government at both national and state level was too weak to combat the power and influence of big business. It was felt that business interests were too materialistic, and that there was a paucity of such values as patriotism and working together for the common good. Business interests often controlled government officials and procedures. **Muckraking journalists** such as Lincoln Steffens felt the answer was in part to reform politics, to increase the power, efficiency and accountability of government at all levels. Ida Tarbell wrote about unfair business practices perpetrated at Standard Oil.

In January 1903 the editor of *McClure's* magazine wrote a hard-hitting editorial in which he attacked powerful political and business interests as immoral and corrupt. The widespread support stimulated other investigations into such areas as diverse as sweatshops and city corruption.

Local and state level

At local levels, reformers tried to mobilise grass roots support to clean up city corruption. For example, often local politicians were paid by **utility companies** to give contracts in which they could charge high prices and offer poor services.
- One solution was to set up regulatory commissions to oversee utilities.

- Another was to elect town councils with professional officials.

By the early 1900s, over 400 urban councils had been reformed.

One of the major reforms at state level was to introduce popularly elected Senators: most Senators had been appointed by state legislatures usually controlled by powerful business interests – railway concerns in California, for example. California was one of the first states to introduce elected Senators – others followed and the process became enshrined in the Seventeenth Amendment of 1915. Also, states increasingly introduced **primaries** so candidates for states and Congress could be selected by local party members rather than powerful interests.

The idea was that increased democracy could reduce political corruption and the power of business interests.

National level

The emphasis here was on reform. However, the measures passed in the late nineteenth century were too vague to be really effective. Democrat President Grover Cleveland had, for example, created the Interstate Commerce Commission in 1887 but it lacked bite. Railroad companies needed to publish their rates and desist from offering preferential rebates to big business, but the commission had no power to regulate the rates themselves. The 1890 Sherman Anti-Trust Act had been easily negated in law (see page 18).

These measures went some way to addressing the power and influence of big business and set precedents for the future, but in themselves they were insufficient to assuage popular feeling. The frustrations people felt led to the creation of the Populist Party and the progressive movement.

Muckraking journalism

Muckraking journalism was the term given to investigative reporting in popular magazines such as *McClure's* and *Collier's* into issues such as scandals in public life and harsh living conditions. These magazines attracted a wide readership; for example, the 1904 edition of *McClure's* sold 750,000 copies. Muckraking journalism helped lead to the development of progressivism (see page 32).

RAG – rate the interpretation

Read the following interpretation and, using three coloured pens, shade the text to show the following:

- Red: Shade anything you disagree with in red.
- Amber: Shade anything you partly agree/disagree with in amber.
- Green: Shade the sections you agree with in green.

EXTRACT 1

From Richard Hofstadter, The Age of Reform, *published in 1968.*

To an extraordinary degree the work of the progressive movement rested upon its journalism. The fundamental critical achievement of American progressivism was the business of exposure, and journalism was the chief occupational source of its creative writers. It is hardly an exaggeration to say that the progressive mind was characteristically a journalistic mind and its characteristic contribution was that of the socially responsible reporter–reformer. The muckraker was a central figure. Before there could be action, there must be information, and exhortation. Grievances had to be given specific objects and these the muckraker supplied. It was muckraking that brought the diffuse malaise of the public into focus.

The practice of exposure itself was not an invention of the muckraking era, nor did muckraking succeed because it had a new idea to offer. The persuasiveness of graft, the presence of a continuous corrupt connection between business and government, the link between government and vice – there was nothing new in the awareness of these things. Since the 1870s exposure had been a recurrent theme in American political life.

 Develop the detail

Below are a sample exam question and a paragraph written in answer to this question. The paragraph contains a limited amount of detail. Annotate the paragraph to add additional detail to the answer.

To what extent were political reforms undertaken to address political corruption in the period 1890 to 1900?

Political reforms to address issues of political corruption were undertaken at local, state and national level. At local level, reforms tried to end political corruption for example by regulating utility companies. At state level, they introduced primaries to elect candidates to political office. At national level, the first anti-trust measures were passed.

Populism and progressivism

The final decade of the nineteenth century and first decade of the twentieth saw the creation of the Populist Party and election of two presidents associated with progressivism – Roosevelt (1901–08) and Taft (1909–13).

Ideas and influence of Bryan

Populism and Bryan

In 1896, Populists gained control of the Democrat Party and installed W.J. Bryan as their candidate in the 1896 presidential election.

The creation of the Populist Party

In 1890 the National Farmers' Alliance (see page 16) created the People's Party, better known as the Populist Party. This was a radical movement which reached out to groups such as black sharecroppers and women; for example, a leading Kansas member, lawyer Mary Elizabeth Lease, advocated direct action by farmers. Populist demands included agricultural reforms (see page 16), graduated income tax, government ownership of railroads and the introduction of a bimetallic currency in which silver coins would be as readily available as gold.

The silver issue

Silver production had grown rapidly in the USA in the last third of the nineteenth century as a result of significant discoveries of lodes in the West. Its value had grown from $156,000 in 1860 to $57 million by 1890. Traditionally the USA had adopted the **gold standard** by which the value of the currency was based on that of gold. This kept the value high. However, bimetallists wanted silver to be used in the manufacture of coins as well as gold – bringing the value down.

The 1890 Sherman Silver Purchase Act had forced the government to purchase 4,500,000 ounces of silver per month for this purpose – but President Cleveland repealed the Act in 1896.

Populists felt the high value of gold led to high interest rates and shortage of credit. The silver issue became their most significant policy. They felt maintaining the gold standard as the sole basis of the value of currency was a classic example of powerful business interests acting in their own interests to the exclusion of other groups.

Fusion with the Democrats

The Populist Party did badly in the 1892 presidential election, with its candidate winning only 22 electoral college votes. Nonetheless, the party remained a force, winning 42 per cent of the vote in the 1894 mid-term congressional elections. However, many of its programmes were supported by the Democrats and adopted by its candidate, W.J. Bryan, in the 1896 presidential election. The Populists agreed to support Bryan.

W.J. Bryan

Bryan was a lawyer from Nebraska with an impassioned style. He was particularly concerned with the silver issue although he embraced all the Populist platform.

The 1896 presidential election

The 1896 presidential election was a contest between the traditional interests of power as exemplified by the Democrats and the radical ideas of Bryan. It was also the first where modern campaigning methods and financing were deployed. The campaign of **William McKinley**, Republican candidate, was managed by Mark Hanna, an unscrupulous political manager who used modern methods such as:

- high-pressure fundraising which raised $3.5 million
- sending out 250 million pieces of campaign literature
- targeting marginal areas with his teams of 1500 speakers.

Bryan travelled over 28,000 kilometres on the campaign trail and gave 600 speeches – but the Republicans spent ten times more and used the media to attack their opponents as unsound, particularly on economics.

McKinley won both the 1896 and 1900 presidential elections, as seen in the table below.

Presidential election results, 1896 and 1900

Year	McKinley – Republican	Bryan – Democrat
1896	7,036,000	6,468,000
1900	7,228,864	6,370,932

McKinley's domestic policies

McKinley's administration appeared to follow traditional policies of *laissez-faire*. There was no significant social reform and in 1897 the Dingley tariff became the most protectionist to date. In the event McKinley's administration was dominated by foreign affairs, but he had little trouble being re-elected in 1900 (see above).

Bryan's policies, however, survived into the progressive movement.

! Summarise the arguments　ａ

Below are a sample exam question and one of the extracts referred to in the question. You must read the extract and identify the interpretation offered. Look for the arguments of the passage.

> Using your knowledge of the historical context, assess how convincing you find the arguments in the extract are in relation to the growth of the Populist movement.

Interpretation offered by the extract:

_____

_____

EXTRACT

From C.P. Hill, 'American Radicalism in the Nineteenth Century', in H.C. Allen and C.P. Hill, British Essays in American History, *published in 1969.*

(Populism) attracted a good deal of support in the South; and it has been pointed out that the embattled American farmers on this occasion were mainly those dependent on the great cash crops, cotton and wheat, whose sales were at the mercy of the world market, and it was an international agrarian crisis which was principally responsible for the growth of Populism in the early 1890s. In the mountain states its main support came from those whose livelihood depended on a third commodity, the world price of which had declined – silver... Its attraction... was never merely economic. At its best, Populism was deeply idealist and humanitarian, blending the traditional agrarian myth at its noblest with that sense of urgency of social reform which was so soon to animate the progressive movement. At its worst, it was credulous, offering an excellent illustration of the American weakness for discovering imaginary conspiracies, this time by the capitalists of Wall Street.

⸙ Complete the paragraph

Below are a sample A-level exam question and a paragraph written in answer to this question.

> How far would you agree that the Populist movement threatened traditional political groupings in the USA in the final decades of the nineteenth century?

The paragraph contains a point and specific examples, but lacks a concluding analytical link back to the question. Complete the paragraph, adding this link back to the question in the space provided.

The Populist movement marked an attempt to widen the political base. It was born out frustrations with the existing two major parties and how they appeared to govern in the interests of the elites often at the expense of other groups – for example, with the emphasis on laissez-faire and high tariffs. However, even when the Populists gained control of the Democrats before the 1896 election and nominated a Populist candidate, W.J. Bryan, the Republicans were able to deploy their vastly superior resources to defeat them. Indeed in 1900 their majority was higher. At the time then the Populists may have posed a threat to the existing political groupings but it seemed that threat had been overcome – although their policies of course survived into, and developed during, the progressive movement of the ensuing decades. Overall then ...

_____

_____

Progressivism and Wilson's New Freedom

Progressivism was a loose term defying close definition. It stood, among other ideas, for reform against corruption, improvement in living conditions, more efficient government, and reducing the power of big business. However, not all progressives supported all of these measures and some may actually have opposed some of them. Nonetheless, historians agree that the first three presidents of the twentieth century were progressive in outlook.

Ideas and influence of Roosevelt

Theodore Roosevelt was McKinley's vice president so took over after the latter's assassination in September 1901. He felt in particular that the federal government needed more powers in order to act effectively as the US developed economically. He introduced a programme of reform known as the Square Deal.

Anti-trust legislation

Roosevelt was particularly opposed to the power of the trusts (see page 18) and sought to use existing legislation more effectively. For example, he used the 1890 Sherman Act to embark on 44 anti-trust prosecutions after succeeding in his attempts to prevent Northern Securities from controlling too many railroads.

Elkins Act, 1903

This empowered the Interstate Commerce Commission to impose heavy fines on both railroad companies who offered rebates to big business concerns, and on the concerns who accepted them.

Hepburn Act, 1906

This empowered the Interstate Commerce Commission still further, giving it authority to set maximum railroad rates and inspect companies' records.

However, opposition, particularly in the Senate, and reluctance to support Commission decisions in the Supreme Court reduced the effectiveness of these laws: the trust lobby was still very powerful.

Arbitration

Roosevelt gained popularity among the working classes for his arbitration in the 1902 anthracite coal strike. Employers had locked out miners demanding better conditions and pay. Roosevelt summoned both sides to Washington and pressurised the employers into coming to an agreement.

Ideas and influence of Taft

Taft was more methodical than Roosevelt, and many felt progressivism lost impetus during his presidency. However, he did promote anti-trust legislation and introduce an eight-hour day for government employees and mine safety legislation.

Wilson's New Freedom

Woodrow Wilson won the 1912 election. He was an academic expert on US government, and committed to reform and modernisation. He called his programme the 'New Freedom'.

Underwood tariff, 1913

In October 1913 the Underwood tariff reduced many customs duties and freed other items entirely. These included wool, food, iron and steel, shoes and machinery. They could all be produced more cheaply in the USA than abroad so didn't need protection from foreign competition.

Loss of government revenue was compensated by the introduction in 1913 of federal income tax.

Federal Reserve Act, 1913

This created for the first time a centralised banking system in the USA. Twelve banking districts were created, each under the supervision of a Federal Reserve Bank. The Federal Reserve Bank in Washington was at the centre of the system.

The centralised system enabled the Federal Reserve Bank to control the monetary supply by setting the rates at which other banks could borrow. It could therefore address **inflation** by restricting borrowing through high interest rates and encourage it in times of **deflation** by reducing it.

Anti-trust legislation

Wilson continued the regulation of big business and giant corporations.

Federal Trade Commission, 1914

This was formed to investigate corporations and 'unfair practices' – although it was weakened by the lack of definition of 'unfair'.

Clayton Anti-Trust Act, 1914

This made certain business practices illegal – such as:
● 'price fixing' to foster monopolies
● 'tying' arrangements whereby retailers were forbidden to handle the products of their main suppliers' rivals.

! Simple essay style

Below is a sample A-level exam question. Use your own knowledge and the information on the opposite page to produce a plan for this question. Choose four general points, and provide three pieces of specific information to support each general point.

Once you have planned your essay, write the introduction and conclusion for it. The introduction should list the points to be discussed in the essay. The conclusion should summarise the key points and justify which point was the most important.

> To what extent did Presidents Roosevelt, Taft and Wilson seek to limit the power of big business and trusts?

⊙ Complete the paragraph

Below are a sample essay question and a paragraph written in answer to this question.

> How far did the presidencies of Roosevelt and Taft mark an end to *laissez-faire* policies?

The paragraph contains a point and specific examples, but lacks a concluding analytical link back to the question. Complete the paragraph, adding this link back to the question in the space provided.

Both Roosevelt and Taft were known as progressive presidents, and Roosevelt in particular sought to break with policies of laissez-faire in many areas. He felt that federal government had been too weak and needed to expand, particularly in relation to the powerful trusts. To this end he began 44 anti-trust prosecutions and supported the 1903 Elkins Act, which strengthened the Interstate Commerce Commission by giving it power to fine railroad companies which offered rebates to big business concerns, and the 1906 Hepburn Act, which allowed it to set maximum rates and examine their records. Taft was less active although he did introduce an eight-hour day for government employees. He initiated few new measures against, for example, trusts. However, there were limits to how far either president broke with the traditions of laissez-faire. For example, neither introduced significant social reform legislation — although Roosevelt did insist on arbitration to end the 1902 coal strike. Overall...

_____

_____

_____

Economic change and developments

The period 1890 to 1920 saw significant economic change and developments in the USA.

The rise of US dominance as an economic and industrial power

The USA developed in terms of production, technology and consumption, all fusing together to create the wealthiest country on earth by the early twentieth century. By 1900 it was almost producing more iron and steel than Britain, Germany and Russia combined.

Production

Capital investment in US manufacturing increased from $1 billion in 1860 to $10 billion by 1900. The value of US manufacturing grew in the same period from $2 billion to $13 billion. By 1914, the USA was producing 33 per cent of the world's manufactured goods.

Technical growth

Between 1860 and 1890, 440,000 patents for new products and processes were taken out in the USA. Most of these had practical purposes; for example, the Bessemer process of steel production helped build steel railroad tracks, ploughs, bridges – and skyscrapers in the cities.

Consumption

The effects of manufacturing growth meant changes in consumption. Products such as cars – 8000 by 1900 – were only for the rich, although by 1888 New York alone had more telephones than in the whole of the UK, and 100,000 Americans had purchased cameras.

However, improved communications especially through railroad growth brought more fresh food to improve the diets of city dwellers and improved production methods meant tinned food became available.

Consequences of US dominance

The USA expanded into foreign investment and production in countries abroad. For example, the value of its exports rose from $1,495,616,000 between 1903 and 1905 to $2,441,252,000 between 1911 and 1915. It also, however, became involved in the economies of both developed and developing countries. In 1950 historian William A. Williams argued that the need for markets was the prime motive for foreign expansion. The need to protect investments and prevent too much foreign competition saw the USA significantly extend its role overseas.

Dollar diplomacy

Dollar diplomacy was the term by which the USA extended its influence in neighbouring countries by use of its economic muscle. For example, in 1911 it took over the management of the Nicaraguan economy when it couldn't pay its foreign debts. It also muscled into a European-based consortium that was financing a major Chinese railway because it realised the value of controlling railroads for economic purposes.

Latin America

US economic investment in Latin America was significant enough to be a major factor in the development of US imperialism (see page 42). For example, by 1900 the USA was investing $50 million in the Cuban economy, while 43 per cent of the value of Mexican economic production was in US hands.

Britain

The USA invested substantially in Britain. Tycoon Charles Tyson Yerkes helped build the London Underground system, particularly the Piccadilly, Northern and Bakerloo lines, and oversaw the introduction of electric power. Heinz opened his first British food factory in Peckham in 1905. Ford cars were being assembled in Britain by 1911. Indeed the level of US investment overall was so great by the early twentieth century that the British press criticised 'an American invasion'.

Open door

In 1899 US Secretary of State John Hay introduced the idea of 'open door' by which states would respect each other's trading rights in China. The point was the USA recognised its economic power and the need to maintain its economic influence. By 1900 the strength of its economic development meant it needed to involve itself in foreign enterprise both to defend its existing investments and in order to continue to expand.

Expansion of sea power

In 1890 and 1892 Captain **Alfred Thayer Mahan** wrote two enormously influential books on the impact of sea power, both to extend national influence and to protect economic interests. Many politicians supported his ideas and during the 1890s the size of the US navy rose from twelfth to fifth largest in the world. The growth of the US navy was increasingly seen as vital in the USA becoming a major world power.

Quick quizzes at **www.hoddereducation.co.uk/myrevisionnotes**

Delete as applicable

Below are a sample exam question and a paragraph written in answer to this question. Read the paragraph and decide which of the possible options (in bold) is most appropriate. Delete the least appropriate options and complete the paragraph by justifying your selection.

'The USA was transformed as a result of economic developments in the period 1890 to 1914.' How far do you agree with this statement?

During the period 1890 to 1914 the USA was transformed to a **great/fair/limited** extent by economic developments. For example, by 1900 it was producing almost more iron and steel than its main European rivals of Britain, Germany and Russia combined. Capital investment increased from $1 billion to $13 billion between 1860 and 1900. Indeed by 1900 the USA produced one-third of all the world's manufactured goods. At home this meant dramatic changes, for example on city landscapes with the development of skyscraper buildings, a national network of railroads which brought fresh food to all regions, thereby improving the diet of many people. However, many goods such as motor cars remained the preserve of the wealthy, while horse and buggy were the main forms of private transport. The country as a whole became much wealthier but for many people life remained non-mechanised and little different as a result of industrialisation. Overall then the extent to which the USA was transformed was **major/moderate/limited**.

 Developing an argument

Below are a sample exam question, a list of key points to be made in the essay, and a paragraph from the essay. Read the question, the plan and the sample paragraph. Rewrite the paragraph in order to develop an argument. Your paragraph should answer the question directly, and set out the evidence that supports your argument. Crucially, it should develop an argument by setting out a general answer to the question and reasons that support this.

To what extent did economic growth in the USA in the period 1890 to 1914 lead to increasing investment and involvement in foreign economies?

Key points

- Growth and strength of US economy.
- Foreign investment.
- Involvement in the economies of developed countries such as Britain.
- Involvement in the economies of developing countries such as Latin America – and the Far East – 'dollar diplomacy' and 'open door' policies.

Sample paragraph

The US economy developed significantly during the period 1890 to 1914. By 1900 in fact it produced one-third of all the world's manufactured goods. The value of its exports grew from $1,495,616,000 between 1903 and 1905 to $2,441,252,000 between 1913 and 1915. It began to invest in countries such as Britain, where one US entrepreneur, Charles Tyson Yerkes, was responsible for building much of the London Underground. It also became involved in developing countries such as in Latin America and the Far East. Here the USA pursued an open door policy to ensure it got its share of trade and investment.

Social developments

The period saw significant social change in the USA both as a result of mass migration and movement into cities.

Mass immigration

Between 1866 and 1915 approximately 15 million people immigrated into the USA mainly from southern and eastern Europe. This was a dramatic change in that earlier European immigration had been mainly focused on the more developed areas of the north and west – or Anglo-Saxon Protestants who reflected the American profile of themselves as a nation.

The peak year for immigration was 1907, with 1,285,000 newcomers – of which eleven times more came from Italy and Russia than in 1882.

Immigration to the USA

Year	Immigrants
1881–1890	5,246,613
1891–1900	3,687,564
1901–1910	8,795,386
1911–1920	5,735,811

Many Americans were worried about this so-called 'new immigration'.

Consequences of mass immigration

- There were fears that the new arrivals did not assimilate into US culture as readily as their northern and western European counterparts, and brought with them alien ideas such as **communism** and **anarchism**.
- There were fears they would undercut wages by working for less than US employees.
- They tended to remain in cities and lived in **ghettos** with their fellows where they maintained their own cultural traditions and language.
- They were accused of having low quality skills and illiteracy – indeed in 1900, 13 per cent of foreign-born Americans were illiterate.
- Many were Catholics which critics saw as anti-American – as though their first loyalty would be to the pope in Rome rather than the flag of the USA.

New immigration was blamed for rises in crime, rises in revolutionary terrorism, rises in anti-US ideas such as trade unionism. Many believed immigrants were inferior to the US ideal of White Anglo-Saxon Protestants (WASPs), and their presence, let alone interracial marriage, would have a negative impact (these marriages or relationships were described as **miscegenation** at the time). There was a common belief in eugenics which taught of racial hierarchies with WASPs at the top and plentiful literature bemoaning the threat new immigrants posed to the white race.

Eugenics and Social Darwinism

Theories of racial inequalities were widely accepted at this time. Eugenics taught there was a hierarchy of racial types. Social Darwinism was concerned with the role of the white races in helping other groups while acknowledging they could never be their equals. The great fear was that miscegenation could see the destruction of the white race.

Urbanisation

The period saw a huge growth in urbanisation. Between 1860 and 1900 the numbers of Americans living in towns of more than 2500 grew from 6 million to 30 million, or 40 per cent of the population. By 1900 there were 38 cities with more than 100,000 population and several cities, notably New York, Boston and Philadelphia, with numbers exceeding 1 million.

There were various reasons for this urbanisation:
- The growth of new immigration.
- The beginnings of the Great Migration of black Americans (see page 40).
- The movement of people from rural to urban areas and subsequent growth of urban areas into formerly rural ones.

Consequences of urbanisation

- Urban areas became centres of manufacture – by 1900, 90 per cent of all goods were manufactured in urban areas.
- An urban culture developed, with more centres of entertainment, sports and leisure. By the 1920s tensions between more traditional rural areas and what were seen as urban centres of vice and unAmerican values were to become significant (see page 68).
- Cities saw technical developments such as improved transport networks, street lighting, electricity, water, gas and sewage systems. The city centre landscape was altered by large buildings such as skyscrapers (see page 16).
- A new urban middle class was developing through the need for administrators, managers, salespeople and so on – from 756,000 in 1870 to 5.6 million by 1910. Often these had emerged from relatively low-income backgrounds so were very optimistic about the future – and prepared to invest in consumer goods, thus fuelling economic growth.

Quick quizzes at **www.hoddereducation.co.uk/myrevisionnotes**

Comparing interpretations

With reference to the two extracts and your understanding of the historical context, which do you find more convincing in relation to immigration and social mobility in the USA in the closing decades of the nineteenth century?

Compare the arguments in the two extracts, and use your contextual knowledge to decide which is more convincing. You could shade the sections of each extract that you agree with.

Then set out the plan of answer identifying agreements between the two extracts, and then disagreements, using your contextual knowledge.

Extract A argument(s)	Extract B argument(s)	Your contextual knowledge
Agreements	Agreements	
Disagreements	Disagreements	

EXTRACT A

From Paul Johnson, A History of the American People, *published in 1997.*

The whole of America was upwardly mobile but New York, for the penniless immigrant, was the very cathedral of ascent. Many immigrants stayed in the tenth ward only a matter of weeks or months. The average Jewish residence in the lower east side as a whole was fifteen years. Then they moved on to Brooklyn, to Harlem (once a wealthy German-Jewish quarter), to the Bronx and Washington heights, then further, and inland. Their children went to universities. Vast numbers became doctors and lawyers. Others set themselves up as small businessmen; then became big businessmen. One-time Jewish peddlers became mail-order tycoons, epitomised by Julius Rosenwald's Sears, Roebuck. The family of Benjamin Bloomingdale from Bavaria, who opened a dry-goods store in 1872, had over 1000 employees in its east side shop by 1888. The Altman Brothers had 16,000 in their store...

The ability of America, led by New York, to transform immigrant millions, most of whom arrived penniless and frightened, into self-confident citizens, wealth-creators and social and cultural assets, was the essential strength of the expanding republic, which had now been doing the same for its own people for the best part of three centuries.

EXTRACT B

From Simon Schama, The American Future, *published in 2009.*

On 11 May 1887, thirteen steamers coming from Liverpool (the *Wyoming*, *Helvetia* and *Baltic*), Antwerp, Marseilles, Le Havre and Bordeaux (the *Chateau d'Yquem*!) unloaded just short of 10,000 on a single day. And the *New York Times* had had enough of the spirit of hospitality... 'Shall we take Europe's paupers, her criminals, her lunatics, her crazy revolutionaries, her vagabonds?' the paper asked. These were labourers 'who lived on garbage' and were a 'standing menace to the city's health'. Another editorial for *The Times* sounded off regularly on the subject and opined that 'in every Anarchist meeting, every official statement concerning the condition of labour or the inmates of our almshouses and asylums for the insane, every report relating to plague spots in the slums of our great cities, may be felt something to remind the people of the United States that immigration under restrictions now provided is not a blessing'.

Seven years later in 1894, the Immigrant Restriction League was duly founded to combat the irresponsible, sentimental universalism (as it saw it) of those who looked upon the torch of liberty (the Statue of Liberty) in New York harbour and wiped a tear from their eye.

The position of African-Americans

The position of African-Americans remained challenging throughout the period 1890 to 1920. Many sought to leave the South for better opportunities in the North, but found only different types of problems.

Life for black Americans in the South

By 1900, most Southern states had disenfranchised African-Americans either by dubious legal means or outright intimidation. Opportunities for African-Americans to improve their lot were limited.

Segregation

All Southern states practised segregation, called 'Jim Crow'. The system was given legal authority in 1896 in the Supreme Court.

Plessy *v.* Ferguson, 1896

This was a Supreme Court ruling which stated that segregation was acceptable so long as facilities were of equal quality. Most whites approved and there was little impetus to define what was meant by equality. Although the Act referred specifically to places of public accommodation – it had been introduced in respect to railway accommodation – it was used to justify separate facilities of all types, from public toilets to service in restaurants.

Terrorism

African-Americans endured discrimination and terrorism. Although the Ku Klux Klan was in abeyance until the 1920s, acts of lynching proliferated – 292 in 1892 alone and almost 5000 between 1882 and 1950. African-Americans had little recourse to the law – local police were notoriously racist.

Education

Where schools existed for African-Americans they tended to be poorly equipped, overcrowded and concentrated by necessity on offering only the most basic education.

Booker T. Washington

One important African-American leader was Booker T. Washington who ran the Tuskagee Institute in Alabama. This was a vocational college, enabling African-American students to become skilled craftsmen. Washington believed:

- African-Americans needed to be taught the skills necessary to become useful citizens

- African-Americans needed the help of whites to improve themselves.

His most famous exposition of this view was in the 'Atlanta Compromise' of 1895. Here he argued that if whites saw African-Americans as economic partners rather than political opponents, the race problem would be resolved. If whites would help African-Americans learn vocational skills, then they would be loyal, hard-working citizens.

Opposition to the Atlanta Compromise

Many whites supported Washington and assisted him in his efforts. He was invited to the White House. Many African-Americans did learn useful vocational skills and improved their lives as a result. However, others felt he had surrendered their dignity and tacitly accepted the idea of white superiority. He remained a controversial figure.

The Great Migration

Many African-Americans moved north in what became known as the Great Migration. However, in the Northern cities they often still found discrimination and limited opportunities.

African-Americans tended to congregate in specific areas of Northern cities such as Harlem in New York which became overcrowded with attendant social problems as a result. In Harlem, for example, the African-American population rose from 50,000 in 1910 to 73,000 by 1920. Migrants found that educational and job opportunities were often limited. However, the presence of so many people in close proximity led to a vibrant culture which saw its flowering in the 1920s in the **Harlem Renaissance**.

W.E. DuBois

DuBois was an intellectual who disagreed significantly with Booker T. Washington. He felt African-Americans should demand their Civil Rights and an end to discrimination. His 'Niagara Movement' – so-called because it had been largely elucidated at the Niagara Conference in 1905 – never gained a widespread following. However, he was partly responsible for the formation of the National Association for the Advancement of Coloured People (NAACP) in 1909, which did become immensely significant in the fight for Civil Rights and equal opportunities.

Below is an extract to read. You are asked to summarise the interpretation about the position of African-Americans in the South in the period 1890 to 1920.

Interpretation offered by the extract:

_____

_____

Counter-argument:

_____

_____

EXTRACT

From C. Vann Woodward, The Strange Career of Jim Crow _(3rd edition), published in 1974._

It would certainly be preposterous to leave the impression that any evidence I have submitted indicates a golden age of race relations in the period between Redemption (the end of Reconstruction) and complete segregation. On the contrary the evidence of race conflict and violence is overwhelming. It was, after all, in the eighties and early nineties that lynching attained the most staggering proportions ever reached in the history of that crime. Moreover the fanatical advocates of racism, whose doctrines of total segregation, disfranchisement and ostracism eventually triumphed over all opposition and became universal practice in the South, were already at work and already beginning to establish dominance over some phases of Southern life. Before their triumph was complete, however, there transpired a period of history whose significance has been neglected. Exploitation there was in that period, as in other periods and in other regions, but it did not follow then that the exploited had to be ostracised. Subordination there was also, unmistakable subordination: but it was not yet an accepted corollary that the subordinates had to be totally segregated and needlessly humiliated by a thousand daily reminders of their subordination.

! **Support or challenge?**

Below is a sample exam question which asks how far you agree with a specific statement. Below this is a series of general statements which are relevant to the question. Using your own knowledge and the information on the opposite page, decide whether these statements support or challenge the statement in the question.

‘The Plessy _v._ Ferguson Supreme Court ruling in 1896 was the most important factor in the segregation of African-Americans from white people in the Southern states in the period 1890 to 1920.’ How far do you agree with this statement?

	Support	Challenge
Segregation in many areas preceded Plessy v. Ferguson.		
Terror was deployed to exclude African-Americans from public life.		
Plessy v. Ferguson insisted on separate but equal facilities.		
Plessy v. Ferguson related specifically to accommodation on public transport.		
The Atlanta Compromise accepted inferior status for African-Americans.		
African-Americans had only limited educational opportunities.		

The period 1890 to 1920 saw the USA become more involved in foreign affairs than at any previous time in its history.

Imperialism

The USA became an imperial power for a variety of reasons.

Economic

The USA had surplus goods for export and needed to protect its growing trade and investments abroad (see page 36). For example, it heavily invested in sugar production in Cuba and Hawaii, and needed naval bases to protect its trade routes to the Far East.

Allied to this was the desire to exploit the resources of less developed countries – the reasoning behind 'dollar diplomacy' and 'open door' policies (see page 36).

White supremacy

The theory of white supremacy was allied to the notion of the 'White Man's Burden' or the responsibility of the civilised races to bring the benefits of their civilisation. President McKinley, for example, argued that the Christianising impulse was his main motivation for annexing the Philippines.

Preclusive imperialism

This suggested that the USA took colonies to prevent others from doing so – particularly Germany which was seeking an Asian empire, for example in Samoa. Samoa itself became divided between the USA and Germany in 1899.

Engagement in international affairs

While the USA was ostensibly neutral in the disputes between the great powers, it gave covert support to Britain and France; for example, at the Algericas Conference of 1906 over foreign interests in Morocco.

The USA also became involved in the Far East and played a leading role in the suppression of the 1900 Boxer rebellion against foreign interests in China.

Annexation of Hawaii

In 1898, the USA annexed Hawaii. This was in part due to various rebellions against the US fruit growers who dominated the governance and economy of the islands, which had been going on throughout the 1890s. President Cleveland had rejected the growers' calls for annexation: McKinley, seeing no end to the conflict, was more amenable.

The Spanish–American–Cuban War, 1898

This war broke out ostensibly because the USA supported the Cubans in their rebellion against their colonial power, Spain. It was sparked by the explosion of the USS vessel *Maine* in Havana, the Cuban capital. Clearly this was mainly an excuse:
- The USA had extensive economic interests in Cuba and wanted to expel the Spanish.
- The **Yellow Press** supported war, citing the Monroe Doctrine (see page 22) and highlighting alleged atrocities by the Spanish authorities.
- Cuban exiles campaigned vigorously for US help.

The impact of the war

The war against Spain was quickly won, but it had escalated into the Far Eastern Spanish colony of the Philippines whose inhabitants were also involved in rebellion.

The Paris Peace Settlement, 1899
- Cuba was granted independence.
- The USA acquired the former Spanish islands of Guam in the Pacific and Puerto Rico in the Caribbean.
- The USA purchased the Philippines for $20 million.

The annexation of the Philippines

The purchase of the Philippines was controversial because it led to a brutal four-year war of subjugation. It was argued the Filipinos were not able to govern themselves, and the USA was morally obliged to raise them to 'civilised' standards. More dubiously, the USA also worried that if they didn't absorb them, another power might.

The Panama Canal

Equally controversial was the building of the Panama Canal to link both sides of the American continent. In 1903 the US government became involved in an independence struggle by Panamanians against their Columbian overlords before any deal was possible. They gave $10 million to the new Panamanian government in return for control of the ten-kilometre Canal Zone. The total cost came to $352 million and the canal wasn't completed until 1914.

! RAG – rate the timeline a

Below are a sample exam question and a timeline. Read the question, study the timeline and, using three coloured pens, put a Red, Amber or Green star next to the events to show:

- Red: Events and policies that have no relevance to the question.
- Amber: Events and policies that have some significance to the question.
- Green: Events and policies that are directly relevant to the question.

'The principal reason why the USA became an imperial power in the period 1890 to 1914 was to defend its economic interests.' How far do you agree with this interpretation?

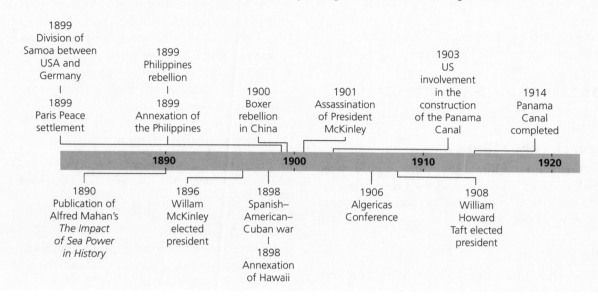

! Eliminate irrelevance a

Below are a sample exam question and a paragraph written in answer to this question. Read the paragraph and identify the parts that are not directly relevant to the question. Draw a line through the information that is irrelevant and justify your deletions in the margin.

To what extent was the desire to extend political and economic influence a major factor in the USA becoming an imperial power in the period 1890 to 1914?

The USA sought to extend both its political and economic influence during the period 1890 to 1914. It had surplus goods for export and needed to protect its growing trade and investments abroad. It had, for example, heavily invested in sugar in Cuba and Hawaii, and needed naval bases to protect its trade routes to the Far East. There was considerable unrest in Hawaii in the 1890s as a result of the growing influence of US growers. In 1890 the McKinley tariff eliminated duties on sugar because US interests controlled the sugar industry in those islands. Similarly the USA had become the largest market for Cuban goods: the total value of US–Cuban trade exceeded $100 million. The USA became embroiled in revolution in Panama because it wanted to complete the canal, which cut through the Panama isthmus and would enable US east coast shipping easy access to the Pacific Ocean and thence to the markets of the Far East. The USA went to war with Spain in part for economic reasons to exclude the latter from the American continent. The Yellow Press had talked up Spanish atrocities to garner public support for the war. Spain was easily defeated.

The USA and the First World War

The USA became involved in the First World War in April 1917 after three years of neutrality.

Neutrality

The USA sought to remain neutral.
- It had remained aloof from European disputes since the early nineteenth century.
- Many of its citizens had ties with Germany or its allies.
- If the USA remained neutral it could trade profitably with all the belligerents.

Reasons for US entry into the war

The situation, however, was far more complex.

Support for the Allies

Most Americans supported the Allies and distrusted German motives. British propaganda showing alleged German atrocities was far more effective than German refutations.

Trade

The USA traded far more with the Allies than with Germany and this was enhanced by the success of the Allied blockade on German ports. In 1914 for example, the USA exported $40 million in munitions to Britain; in 1916 it was $1.29 billion.

Unrestricted submarine warfare

Germany practised unrestricted submarine warfare, sinking all ships en route to Britain. It hoped it could thereby starve Britain of supplies and food. Americans were incensed by the sinking of the British liner *Lusitania* in February 1915, with the loss of 128 Americans among the 1100 dead. While Germany agreed not to attack US ships as a result, it rescinded the decision in January 1917.

The Zimmerman Note

In March 1917 British intelligence meanwhile intercepted the Zimmerman Note in which Germany offered to support Mexico if it went to war to win back its lost territories (see page 22).

By 1917, Russia was being defeated by Germany. The USA feared the Allies might be defeated if Germany moved its victorious forces west to supplement its existing troops.

The USA felt it had no choice but to declare war in April 1917.

Impact of entry into the war

The impact on US entry into the war was profound:
- The growth of government was rapid.
- The war cost $33.5 billion. Two-thirds of this was raised by loans such as Liberty and Victory loans where people were invited to invest in loans to pay for the war effort.
- The federal government raised income tax – in 1918 the highest level was 77 per cent compared to 7 per cent in 1913. One-third of the cost of the war was raised by taxation.
- The railroads were run as a single co-ordinated system to facilitate the efficient movement of troops and supplies.

Wartime governance

In spring 1918, Congress gave President Wilson draconian powers over the political and economic life of the nation:
- A War Industries Board was set up to control and direct the war effort.
- Massive incentives were given to farmers to take more land into production; food exports to Allied countries tripled in size.
- The 1917 Espionage Act made it illegal to send literature deemed seditious or opposing the war effort through the US mail. It could be punishable by 20 years' imprisonment or fines of up to $10,000. Critics said the Espionage Act was too imprecise: the 1918 Sedition Act strengthened it.
- The 1918 Sedition Act made it illegal to criticise the government or the USA.

The Great Migration

The Great Migration of African-Americans from the South to the Northern cities gathered pace. More than 500,000 moved to find war work during the years 1914 to 1918. The African-American population of New York rose from 92,000 to 152,000 and that of Detroit from 5000 to 41,000.

Women

There was no mass mobilisation of women for the war effort. Their role was mainly limited to selling war bonds and sending comforts to the troops abroad. Only 6000 were engaged in aircraft manufacture. Labour unions opposed the wartime recruitment of women because they felt they would depress wages.

How far do you agree?

Read the extract below and summarise each of its arguments. Use your knowledge to agree or contradict.

Arguments in extract	Knowledge that corroborates	Knowledge that contradicts
1		
2		
3		

EXTRACT

From Adam I.P. Smith, 'The Great American U Turn', in BBC History magazine, published in April 2017.

When Wilson changed his mind about American engagement, he did so because he felt he had run out of other options. This was no longer a war of choice, he thought, but a conflict that had been forced upon him.

He didn't know it at the time but the final chain of events that led him to that conclusion began on 8 January 1917. On that day the German High Command ordered the resumption of unrestricted submarine warfare in the Atlantic. Battered by the Somme offensive on the western front the Germans were on the point of being forced to withdraw their forces to the relative security of the Hindenburg Line. Seemingly unable to win the war by conventional means, the German government gambled on being able to win it by cutting off Britain's Atlantic supply route – even at what they must have known would be the almost certain price of American entry.

Wilson had staked much on his efforts to pose as disinterested mediator; the resumption of U-boat attacks on neutral shipping was a rebuff to his peace efforts as well as a direct threat to US interests. When the new German policy became known, Wilson severed diplomatic relations and, soon after, ordered the arming of US merchant vessels.

And then, in early March, the administration revealed to the press the contents of a decoded telegram from the German foreign minister Arthur Zimmermann to the Mexican president suggesting a military alliance.

Spectrum of importance

Below are an essay title and a list of general points which could be used to answer it. Use your own knowledge and the information on the opposite page to reach a judgement about the importance of these general points to the question posed. Write numbers on the spectrum below to indicate their relative importance. Having done this, write a brief justification of your placement, explaining why some of these factors are more important than others. The resulting diagram could form the basis of an essay plan.

'The resumption of unrestricted submarine warfare was the most important reason for the USA entering the First World War in 1917.' How far do you agree with this statement?

1 Maintenance of trade with the allies

2 Resumption of unrestricted submarine warfare

3 Zimmermann telegram

4 Wilson's failed peace initiatives

5 Fear that the Allies might be defeated

6 Desire to influence the peace agreements

Least important ←——————————————————————→ Most important

The USA emerged from the war stronger and more powerful than ever before. It added to the significant changes which had come about since 1890.

Economic power

The USA emerged the leading creditor nation because it had lent billions to the Allies and other nations during the war. By 1917 alone it was owed $2.25 billion by the Allies. It had, moreover, expanded its industrial capacity to manufacture goods: by 1918 it had overtaken Germany as the world's leading producer of fertilisers and chemicals. Other countries which had relied on Britain and France for goods or investment now turned to the USA. This can be seen in the following table showing US investment in Latin America in millions of dollars.

Country	1913	1929
Argentina	40	611
Bolivia	10	133
Brazil	50	476
Chile	15	396
Colombia	2	260
Ecuador	10	25
Paraguay	3	15
Peru	35	151
Uruguay	5	64
Venezuela	3	162

Social and ethnic divisions

The 1920 census showed more than 50 per cent of Americans were living for the first time in urban areas: 54 million out of 106 million. However, one should not overemphasise this fact; 16 of the 54 million still lived in communities of fewer than 25,000 inhabitants and many still held on to 'traditional' values such as thrift, hard work and plain living.

Nevertheless, the USA was becoming more cosmopolitan and diverse. The waves of new immigrants and influx of African-Americans had changed the nature of many urban areas and developed their own cultures – this would be shown in the 1920s, for example in the popularity of jazz music.

Ethnic divisions remained – indeed were exacerbated. The movement of African-Americans into cities in the war years had caused considerable tensions, such as the riots in the city of East St Louis in summer 1917 which saw 39 deaths.

Political reaction to the growth in government

Political reaction was often tense. There was widespread distrust of the expansion of government which had been perceived during the presidencies of Roosevelt, Taft and Wilson but particularly during the war years. Many Republicans sought to reverse these, favouring a return to *laissez-faire*. The Republican candidate in the 1920 election, Warren Harding, promised 'a return to normalcy', by which he meant non-involvement abroad and reduction in the role of government. In the election, with Wilson incapacitated by a stroke, Harding won with a clear majority of 16 million votes to 9 million.

Foreign involvement

The USA and Wilson in particular became heavily involved in the peace process, although it was disillusion here that was to lead to an attempted return to isolationism in the 1920s.

Renewed isolationism

There was a strong sense that the USA had bailed out the Allies and won the war on their behalf. Many Americans sought a return to non-involvement in European affairs or even isolationism. This was exemplified:
- by the Senate rejecting the peace treaties which it felt could simply lead to another war
- by refusing to participate in the League of Nations, a new international organisation set up to prevent future wars.

However, it was impossible for the USA with its economic power and influence to adopt a policy of isolationism. Throughout the ensuing decades it became involved in disarmament conferences and treaties and continued its policies of intervention, particularly in Latin America, to protect its economic interests.

Turning assertion into argument

Below are a series of definitions, an essay title and two sample conclusions. One of the conclusions achieves a high mark because it contains an argument. The other achieves a lower mark because it contains only description and assertion. Identify which is which. The mark scheme on page 7 will help you.

- **Description**: a detailed account.
- **Assertion**: a statement of fact or an opinion which is not supported by a reason.
- **Reason**: a statement which explains or justifies something.
- **Argument**: an assertion justified with a reason.

To what extent were political, social and ethnic divisions evident in the USA in 1920?

Student 1

There were considerable political, social and ethnic divisions in the USA in 1920. The 1920 census showed more than 50 per cent of Americans lived for the first time in urban areas: 54 million out of 106 million. The USA was becoming more cosmopolitan and diverse. During the First World War half a million African-Americans migrated to find work and a better life in the industrial cities of the North. This caused tensions such as the riots in the city of East St Louis in summer 1917 which saw 39 deaths.

Political tensions focused on those who opposed the growth in government of the progressive and wartime years and those who wished to turn back the clock. Republicans promised a return to laissez-faire.

Student 2

There were considerable political, social and ethnic tensions in the USA by 1920. Politically many had grown disillusioned by the growth in government in the progressive and wartime years and sought to redress the balance. Republicans in particular advocated a return to laissez-faire and a retrenchment in government activity. They also felt the USA had rescued the Allies during the war and now sought a return to non-involvement in foreign entanglements. Social divisions remained and the war in particular had resulted in considerable dislocation as exemplified by the half a million African-Americans who moved to the Northern cities in search of greater opportunities. Tensions between the races led to riots, for example in East St Louis in 1917 when 39 African-Americans died.

Recommended reading

- Niall Ferguson, *Colossus* (2003), Chapter 1
- John B. Judis, *The Folly of Empire: What George W. Bush Could Learn from Theodore Roosevelt* (2004), Chapters 3 and 4
- C. Vann Woodward, *The Strange Career of Jim Crow* (3rd edition, 1974), pages 31–111
- Warren Zimmermann, *The First Great Triumph: How Five Americans Made Their Country a World Power* (2002), Introduction; Part 2

Exam focus (AS-level)

Below are two extracts and a sample AS question and Level 5 answer on interpretations.

With reference to these extracts (A and B) and your understanding of the historical context, which of these two extracts provides the more convincing interpretation of the reasons why the USA sought an empire during the presidencies of McKinley and Roosevelt?

EXTRACT A

From Warren Zimmermann, The First Great Triumph: How Five Americans Made Their Country a World Power, *published in 2002.*

With a propitious intellectual and cultural climate, a burgeoning economy, a swelling self-confidence and the preparatory activity of several vigorous Secretaries of State, the United States seemed overdue for imperial adventure. But why was it so long in coming? Three elements were lacking and were not supplied until the 1890s: military power, a political consensus, and an imperial opportunity...

The United States did not have a navy that could sustain expansion overseas until late in the century... it would not have been capable of taking and holding any territory contested by another power. But by 1898, as a result of a sustained shipbuilding programme begun in the 1880s, the US Navy was among the best in the world...

As the century drew to a close, Congress, enlarged by representatives of new states that themselves exemplified American expansionism, became more amenable to assertive politics. In parallel, as the country and its economy grew, the executive branch and the federal bureaucracy became more necessary to the effective functioning of government and therefore more powerful.

In 1895, with possibilities becoming more favourable for a burst of imperialism, a revolution against Spanish rule in Cuba provided the opportunity.

EXTRACT B

From John B. Judis, The Folly of Empire: What George W. Bush Could Learn from Theodore Roosevelt, *published in 2004.*

American proponents of imperialism argued that the country needed colonies to boost its military power and find markets for its capital, but they also believed that by expanding overseas, the United States was fulfilling its historical mission to transform the world in its image. The United States had been founded by descendants of emigrants from Protestant Britain and Holland who viewed their new land as 'a city on a hill' that would initiate a new Israel and the 'Kingdom of God on Earth'. Well after the glow of the Puritan conviction dimmed, Americans still believed that they had a unique or special millennial role in the transforming of the world... into states and countries that shared America's commitment to liberty and democracy. Roosevelt, McKinley and the other proponents of an American imperialism insisted that by annexing other countries, America would, in McKinley's words, 'civilise and Christianise them'.

Both of the extracts are useful for explaining reasons why the USA sought an empire during the presidencies of McKinley and Roosevelt, but I found Extract A slightly more convincing because it covered more ground. Extract B gave one reason while Extract A offered a wider discussion.

Valid judgement in introduction.

Extract A highlights the timing of the presidencies of McKinley and Roosevelt: while there had been an increasing will towards imperialism in preceding years, it was only during the period of their presidencies that three crucial factors came together – the growth of the navy, the development of political agreement between Congress and the presidency that imperialism was desirable, and most crucially of all perhaps, the opportunity, in this case the Cuban rebellion against Spain. Both the quest for empire and circumstances to facilitate it had been developing over the previous years. US economic interests in Cuba for example had been growing for some time and by 1895 the USA provided the largest market for Cuban exports: indeed the total value of Cuban–US trade exceeded $100 million. Naval expansion had been stimulated by the two books written by Captain Alfred Mahan in the early 1890s which showed that naval power was a key to national expansion: although it was more in the 1890s than 1880s that naval expansion really developed. The extract is convincing in that it was during the period of the presidencies of McKinley and Roosevelt that imperialism did develop; McKinley's predecessor Grover Cleveland, for example, had refused to annex Hawaii while McKinley did so in 1898. Of course the factors Zimmermann describes did not happen in isolation, naval expansion had been on the agenda and naval secretaries had called for development in the 1880s, while federal government had been growing more assertive during the first presidency of Grover Cleveland. However, the fact that these three factors did come together at the time they did to stimulate the growth of imperialism is persuasive; it was the timing of Cuban rebellion, largely outside the control of the US for example which presented the opportunity for the war against Spain.

Shows understanding of the extract.

Good use of contextual knowledge.

Engages with argument in extract.

Extract B examines a further reason for the growth of imperialism: the impulse that countries would be better as a result of their contact with United States. This embraced a variety of factors such as the desire to Christianise and civilise, to bring native peoples up to the level of Americans. This has its foundation in issues of Manifest Destiny, and the belief that Americans were blessed by God with the finest systems of governance and society in the world, and it was their duty to share them with those countries less fortunate. It was a genuinely held belief. McKinley cited it directly as his reason for annexing the Philippines in 1899. Clearly, however, in emphasising this one reason in this extract, there is no mention of others such as the need to control new markets or to protect existing US interests. Roosevelt also was more cynical in protecting American interests, as for example with his interventions in Latin America such as the control of the Dominican Republic's custom service in 1903 to ensure that country paid its debts.

Valid contextual knowledge.

Critical engagement with extract content.

The extracts give convincing reasons for the reasons why the USA sought an empire during the presidencies of McKinley and Roosevelt. Extract A is particularly useful in showing that the impulse was controversial and there was considerable disagreement. Extract B explains how the underlying factors may have been present but the timing must also be right – it discusses the three triggers. However, neither really explains the importance of economic factors and trade. They also omit to mention the argument for preclusive imperialism – that one country might take particular colonies to prevent others from doing so. However, they are convincing in that both of them go beyond specific reasons to look at wider issues – the timing and extent of agreement as to the desirability of imperialism.

Summarises extracts in terms of question.

Explains omissions.

This is a very good answer which engages critically with the extracts to show excellent understanding of their arguments and omissions. There is precise contextual understanding. This would achieve Level 5.

Find the evidence

The most important element in producing an argument is supporting evidence and examples. Read the answer again and identify where evidence has been used effectively to support a point.

Exam focus (A-level)

Below is Extract C and a sample essay. It was written in response to an A-level question. Read it and the comments around it.

Using your understanding of the historical context, assess how convincing the arguments in these extracts (A, B and C) are in relation to the reasons why the USA sought an empire during the presidencies of McKinley and Roosevelt.

EXTRACT C

From Niall Ferguson, Colossus, *published in 2004.*

... two related things made the American experiment with empire different from its transatlantic counterpart [Britain]. First the political base for imperialism was narrower: empire appealed much more to the elites of the industrial North than to the rest of the country. Secondly the economic rationale for acquiring colonies was more open to doubt. Britain had embraced free trade as early as the 1840s... the bankers of the City of London, whose business it was to direct British capital overseas, had a vested interest in a situation of both free trade and empire. How could the debtor countries of the New World be expected to honour their obligations if their exports of primary products did not have free access to the British market?... In the United States there were men who made similar arguments but there were more powerful protectionist lobbies pushing in the opposite direction. Their argument was that the United States had no need of British style colonies if their function was simply to inundate the America market with goods that America could just as well produce for themselves (albeit less cheaply). Other opponents, dismayed at the changing complexion of immigrants coming to the United States, saw colonies as just a further source of inferior racial stock.

Extract A highlights the timing of the presidencies of McKinley and Roosevelt: while there had been an increasing will towards imperialism in preceding years, it was only during the period of their presidencies that three crucial factors came together – the growth of the navy, the development of political agreement between Congress and the presidency that imperialism was desirable, and most crucially of all perhaps, the opportunity, in this case the Cuban rebellion against Spain. Both the quest for empire and circumstances to facilitate it had been developing over the previous years. US economic interests in Cuba, for example, had been growing for some time and by 1895 the USA provided the largest market for Cuban exports: indeed the total value of Cuban–US trade exceeded $100 million. Naval expansion had been stimulated by the two books written by Captain Alfred Mahan in the early 1890s which showed that naval power was a key to national expansion: although it was more the 1890s than 1880s in which naval expansion really developed. The extract is convincing in that it was during the period of the presidencies of McKinley and Roosevelt that imperialism did develop; McKinley's predecessor Grover Cleveland, for example, had refused to annex Hawaii while McKinley did so in 1898. Of course the factors Zimmermann describes did not happen in isolation, naval expansion had been on the agenda and naval secretaries had called for development in the 1880s, while federal government had been growing more assertive during the first presidency of Grover Cleveland. However, the fact that these three factors did come together at the time they did to stimulate the growth of imperialism is persuasive; it was the timing of Cuban rebellion, largely outside the control of the US for example which presented the opportunity for the war against Spain. Overall, Extract A is particularly useful in showing that the impulse was controversial and there was considerable disagreement.

Shows understanding of the extract.

Good use of contextual knowledge.

Engages with argument in extract.

Quick quizzes at **www.hoddereducation.co.uk/myrevisionnotes**

Extract B examines a further reason for the growth of imperialism: the impulse that countries would be better as a result of their contact with United States. This embraced a variety of factors such as the desire to Christianise and civilise, to bring native peoples up to the level of Americans. This has its foundation in issues of Manifest Destiny, and the belief that Americans were blessed by God with the finest systems of governance and society in the world, and it was their duty to share it with those countries less fortunate. It was a genuinely held belief. McKinley cited it directly as his reason for annexing the Philippines in 1899. Clearly, however, in emphasising this one reason in this extract, there is no mention of others such as the need to control new markets or to protect existing US interests. Roosevelt also was more cynical in protecting American interests, as for example with his interventions in Latin America such as the control of the Dominican Republic's custom service in 1903 to ensure that country paid its debts.

Valid contextual knowledge.

Critical engagement with extract content.

Extract C gives a more nuanced view of the imperialist impulse, showing it was not universally held in the USA. Ferguson asserts that the desire for imperialism appealed more to the Northern industrial interests, and it was clearly driven by a desire to protect their economic interests. He also gives the example of Britain which saw the need to encourage trade with colonies so they could afford to pay their debts – which may be a more satisfactory solution than taking over their customs service or invading them. However, Ferguson does not consider trade as a crucial factor in the way for example William A. Williams did.

Ferguson shows the desire for imperialism was not shared by all. Many saw colonies as an unnecessary burden, and indeed sought to discourage trade. Many Americans supported protection as exemplified by the high 1890 McKinley tariff which increased duties on many manufactured goods by as much as 50 per cent. There was also a racist impulse which feared imperialism would introduce into the USA peoples deemed to be inferior – at a time when there were widespread concerns about the 'new immigration' from southern and eastern Europe and its impact.

Explains crucial point in extract.

This is a very good answer which engages critically with the extracts to show excellent understanding of their arguments and omissions. There is precise contextual understanding. This would achieve Level 5.

Find the evidence

The most important element in producing an argument is supporting evidence and examples. Read the answer again and identify where evidence has been used effectively to support a point.

Domestic politics in the 1920s

Harding, Coolidge and Republican conservatism

Republicans monopolised the White House during the 1920s. Domestically their agenda was to reduce federal government activity and spending. This was in keeping with the characteristics of the age: *laissez-faire* economics and prosperity.

The presidency of Warren Harding, 1921–23

President Harding was a small-town newspaper editor who many felt was out of place in the White House. However, his administration did enjoy some successes:

- He appointed many able men to government roles, such as financial wizard Andrew Mellon as Treasury Secretary and **Herbert Hoover**, a proven excellent administrator as Secretary of Commerce.
- He was elected to reduce government spending, which had risen tenfold to $5 billion between 1910 and 1920. The Budget and Accounting Act of 1921 required government departments to present budgets for presidential approval: by 1922 expenditure had fallen to $3.373 billion and Mellon was able to reduce taxes.
- He supported the Sheppard–Towner Maternity Aid Act which gave federal monies to support infant and maternity health programmes.

Harding died in office in 1923, to be replaced by his vice president Calvin Coolidge.

The presidency of Calvin Coolidge, 1923–28

Coolidge epitomised the *laissez-faire* presidency. He encouraged business untrammelled by government interference. He reduced taxes on three separate occasions, but despite this his government ran at a profit: $677 million in 1925 and $603 million two years later. Mellon meanwhile gave tax reductions worth $3.5 billion to large-scale industrial concerns. By 1928, 98 per cent of Americans paid no federal taxes. While this may have been popular, the downside was that the federal government actually did very little within the USA.

Laissez-faire government

Coolidge's domestic policies may be characterised more by what they didn't do than what they did. Government economies meant fewer regulations and fewer personnel to enforce them. As a result organisations such as the Federal Trade Commission could not operate effectively. Existing laws concerning sharp business practices such as price fixing were often ignored.

President Hoover

Herbert Hoover, a well-respected public servant, was elected president in 1928. He was hugely optimistic about the economy – in his inaugural speech he insisted poverty had been defeated in the USA. However, within two years the Wall Street Crash of October 1929 ushered in the Great Depression which destroyed such optimism and the efficacy of *laissez-faire* politics.

Republican conservatism

Many Republicans held conservative views and disliked any government intervention in the economy. Financiers like Andrew Mellon believed if business was allowed to continue without regulation, it would thrive. They felt government interference stifled innovation and industrial progress. As business grew more wealthy and more people were employed, they believed wealth would percolate down to all classes. Their views were supported by the fact that, during the 1920s, unemployment never exceeded 3.7 per cent and inflation was never higher than 1 per cent. Real wages of industrial workers rose by 14 per cent between 1914 and 1929.

It seemed that the USA was enjoying real wealth and prosperity as a result in part of *laissez-faire* and government non-interference. Coolidge's successor, Herbert Hoover, said in his inaugural address that the USA had never been so prosperous. However, this prosperity was not to continue.

ⓘ Introducing and concluding an argument

Look at the key points of the answer below.

1 How good is the proposed introduction?

2 How effective is the proposed conclusion?

3 Could either be improved – especially in relation to Level 5 answers?

To what extent were the *laissez-faire* policies pursued by the Republican presidents of the 1920s mainly in the interests of big business?

Key points

- Political scandals
- Tax reductions as a result of reduced government activities
- 1920s prosperity
- Lack of legislation to reduce social ills such as child labour
- Immigration laws
- Theory of Wealth percolating down

Introduction

It appeared that the laissez-faire policies of the Republican governments operated mainly in the interests of big business. However, many of those who benefited would have agreed with Treasury Secretary Andrew Mellon that wealth filtered down, so what was in the interests of big business was ultimately in the interests of everyone else in society. Laissez-faire policies seemed to offer what many Americans required in the 1920s as the economy appeared prosperous. However, they also meant that there was no legislation to combat undoubted social ills such as child labour and indeed reductions in government meant there was less enforcement of those regulations that did exist.

Conclusion

The Republican presidents then did as little as possible. This meant less government which in turn meant large tax reductions — especially for big business. However, laissez-faire policies worked only in the interests of big business. Ordinary people needed government support — for example, there were few laws against them being exploited by unscrupulous employers. Laissez-faire policies also concealed that the unregulated economy was unsound — and in October 1929 the Wall Street Crash ushered in the Great Depression.

ⓘ Develop the detail

Below are a sample essay title and a paragraph written in answer to this question. The paragraph contains a limited amount of detail. Annotate the paragraph to add additional detail to the answer.

'The Republican governments of the 1920s acted primarily in the interests of the wealthy.' Assess the validity of this statement.

The Republican presidents of the 1920s pursued laissez-faire policies which operated primarily in the interests of the wealthy. They reduced government activity for example, which meant tax reductions. Less government activity meant even those few laws which did regulate issues such as unfair business practices were not investigated. There were no laws to protect vulnerable groups. However, political scandals did come to light and the perpetrators were punished.

Hoover and the Depression

The Great Depression

Between 1929 and 1933, economic depression spread throughout the USA, caused by the Wall Street Crash (see page 62) in 1929. Unemployment grew from 1,550,000 or 3.14 per cent of the labour force in 1929 to 12,830,000 or 24.75 per cent by 1933. National wealth as defined in terms of **Gross Domestic Product (GDP)** showed a significant decline during the Depression. The GDP fell from $107.8 billion in 1929 to $56.2 billion in 1933.

The responses of President Hoover

Hoover recognised the scale of the Depression but believed people should help themselves. His response was a mixture of **voluntarism** and indirect aid through loans to industry and states.

Government measures

International trade

Hoover's initial reaction was to protect US industry from foreign competition. In July 1930 he signed the Smoot–Hawley tariff which had been introduced in Congress. It was the highest tariff in US history, with 40 per cent on both industrial and agricultural imports. The result was a devastating fall in international trade of $1.2 billion by 1931. The tariff harmed both US industrialists whose foreign clients could no longer afford to buy US goods and US farmers who needed to sell their huge surpluses abroad.

However, having passed this to protect US commerce, Hoover also sought in part to remedy its impact by the repudiation of **war debts**.

Repudiation of war debts

As the Depression spread throughout the world, Hoover announced in June 1931 that the USA would postpone the collection of war debts for 18 months. This was designed to help countries begin to trade again – although it did to solve the problems caused by the Smoot–Hawley tariff and in any event most countries remained too poor to see any resurgence in international trade.

Unemployment relief

Hoover secured $500,000 from Congress in 1932 to help charities and relief agencies, and set up the President's Emergency Relief Committee to help them co-ordinate their efforts.

Federal Home Loan Bank Act, June 1932

This was intended to save mortgages by making credit easier, thereby avoiding evictions. Federal Loan banks were set up to help loan associations provide mortgages. However, these loans were no more than 50 per cent of the value of the property and therefore often inadequate to prevent homes being repossessed due to non-payment of mortgages.

The Reconstruction Finance Corporation, July 1932

The Reconstruction Finance Corporation (RFC) was established to lend up to $2 billion to banks, railroads and other financial institutions in trouble. However, critics said most of the monies went to the largest institutions – indeed 50 per cent of the loans went to the seven largest banks.

The government argued that it made sense to help the largest firms remain solvent as they were the biggest employers. However, many felt that the RFC helped powerful institutions but did nothing for the people who really needed help – the unemployed and dispossessed. It was pressure from these voices that was influential finally in the provision of some form of relief.

Emergency Relief and Construction Act, 1932

The Emergency Relief and Construction Act was set up in the summer of 1932 and authorised the RFC to lend up to $1.5 billion to states to finance public works which could provide employment. However, to be eligible, states had to be bankrupt and the projects would have to generate enough revenue to pay off the loans.

While some conservative critics said Hoover was intervening too much and the Depression would right itself if left alone, most felt he had not done enough and would not be voting for him in the 1932 presidential election.

Reasons for the ineffectiveness of Hoover's responses

Although he was to intervene more than any other president, the measures he took were inadequate to address the scale of the Depression and he could not countenance direct government relief.

He refused direct government intervention even when a severe drought saw near starvation conditions in the South in 1930–31. Congress in fact allocated only $47 million to alleviate distress there, and even that was in the form of loans which had to be repaid.

! Summarise the arguments

Below are an essay title and one of the extracts referred to in the question. You must read the extract and identify the interpretation offered. Look for the arguments of the passage.

> With reference to the extract and your contextual knowledge, how convincing do you find the extract in relation to the effectiveness of Hoover's efforts to end the Depression which began in 1929?

Interpretation offered by the extract:

_____

EXTRACT

From Paul Johnson, A History of the American People, *published in 1997.*

When the magnitude of the crisis became apparent later in the year [1929] Andrew Mellon, the Treasury Secretary, at least spoke out to repudiate Hoover's interventionist policy and return to strict *laissez-faire*. He told Hoover that administration policy should be to 'liquidate labour, liquidate stocks, liquidate the farmers, liquidate real estate' and so 'purge the rottenness from the economy'. It was the only sensible advice Hoover received throughout his presidency. By allowing the Depression to let rip, unsound businesses would quickly have been bankrupted and the sound would have survived. Wages would have fallen to their natural level. That for Hoover was the rub. He believed that high wages were the most important element in prosperity and that maintaining wages at existing levels was essential to contain and overcome depressions.

From the very start therefore Hoover agreed to take on the business cycle and stamp it flat with all the resources of government... he resumed credit inflation, the Federal Reserve adding almost $300 million to credit in the last week of October 1929 alone.

! RAG – rate the factors a

Below are a sample exam question and a list of factors. Read the question, study the timeline and, using three coloured pens, put a Red, Amber or Green star next to the events to show:

- Red: Events and policies that have no relevance to the question.
- Amber: Events and policies that have some significance to the question.
- Green: Events and policies that are directly relevant to the question.

> 'The scale of the Depression was too great for President Hoover's policies to be effective.' Assess the validity of this statement.

Factors

1928 Kellogg–Briand pact

1928 Hoover's electoral victory

1929 The Wall Street Crash

1929 to 1933 Unemployment grew by 3.14 per cent to 24.75 per cent

1930 Smoot–Hawley tariff raised tariffs

1931 Repudiation of war debts

1932 President's Emergency Relief Committee

1932 Federal Home Loan Bank Act

1932 Reconstruction Finance Corporation

1932 Emergency Relief and Reconstruction Act

1932 Hoover defeated in the presidential election

F.D. Roosevelt and the New Deal, 1933–35

Franklin Delano Roosevelt was elected president in 1932. He promised a '**New Deal**' to restore faith in the US economy through the goals of relief, recovery and reform. However, there was no specific blueprint about how this would be achieved and Roosevelt was a **fiscal conservative** committed to a balanced budget. Roosevelt was charismatic, appealing to people via '**fireside chats**' on the radio and engendering confidence in his policies.

The First New Deal

The Hundred Days

The first hundred days of Roosevelt's presidency saw more legislation than at any previous time in US history. In particular, emergency legislation was passed and '**alphabet agencies**' set up to deal with the problems of the Depression.

Banking and finance

Banking and finance were reformed to make them stronger and restore public confidence.
- The Emergency Banking Relief Act (EBRA) gave the Treasury the authority to investigate banks threatened with collapse and authorised the Reconstruction Finance Corporation to buy up their debts. This was subsequently strengthened by the Glass–Steagall Act which insured bank deposits against bank failure.
- The stock exchange was regulated through the Securities Exchange Commission which oversaw market activities and prevented fraudulent activities such as **insider dealing**.

Emergency relief

The Federal Emergency Relief Administration (FERA) was set up in May 1933. It was given $500 million divided equally among states to provide relief for the unemployed. Half was given directly by FERA to the states and half kept back, to give them $1 for every $3 of their own funds they spent on relief.

Roosevelt hoped to make the emergency relief measures self-financing and they were often started with loans. It was hoped these would be repaid as, for example, public works projects went into profit.

Alphabet agencies

Sixteen 'alphabet agencies' were set up to deal with specific issues relating to recovery from the Depression and relief for those affected by it.

Help for farmers

Agricultural problems such as overproduction were dealt with by the Agricultural Adjustment Agency (AAA) which paid farmers to produce less. It was hoped this would solve the problems of overproduction and see prices rise as a result of reduced output. More contentious was the slaughter of 6 million piglets to enable the price of pork to rise.

On the surface the agency was successful in that prices of produce affected rose. For example, the price of cotton rose from 6.5 cents per pound in 1932 to 10 cents in 1933, while total farm income rose from $4.5 billion in 1932 to $6.9 billion two years later.

Help for industry

The National Industry Recovery Act (NIRA) set up the National Recovery Administration to facilitate industrial recovery. Firms were encouraged to agree to codes establishing:
- working conditions
- product standards.

Public works

The second part of the NIRA was the Public Works Administration, funded with $3.3 billion with the aim of **pump-priming**. It was hoped that expenditure on public works such as road building would stimulate the economy and create permanent jobs. However, it was found that many of its employees went back on relief when their contracts ended. In this sense the scheme offered temporary relief for many of the unemployed but was less successful in stimulating permanent recovery.

Civilian Conservation Corps

Roosevelt understood that young people needed to gain experience of work. The Civilian Conservation Corps was formed to provide them with useful jobs, in conservation in national parks, forests and public lands, for example. By 1935 it had 500,000 recruits: among its work was the installation of 65,100 miles of telephone lines in inaccessible areas and the planting of 3 billion trees. It gave countless young men a new sense of self-respect and comradeship.

The impact of the First New Deal

The First New Deal had a huge political impact:
- For the first time the government gave direct relief.
- Roosevelt helped to restore confidence in the economy.
- Overall the funding was insufficient for the scale of the problem, but it set an important precedent about the role and responsibilities of federal government which would endure until the late twentieth century.

Support or challenge?

Below is a sample essay title which asks how far you agree with a specific statement. Below this is a series of general statements which are relevant to the question. Using your own knowledge and the information on the opposite page, decide whether these statements support or challenge the statement in the question.

To what extent did the First New Deal transform the role of federal government?

	Support	Challenge
Roosevelt was a fiscal conservative who aimed to balance the budget.		
The first hundred days of his administration saw the creation of alphabet agencies.		
Banking and finance was reformed.		
The Agricultural Adjustment Act paid farmers to produce less.		
Public works schemes were initiated to reduce unemployment.		
Roosevelt believed in working with private industry, for example in the NRA.		

RAG – rate the interpretation

Read the following interpretation and, using three coloured pens, shade the text to show the following:
- Red: Shade anything you disagree with in red.
- Amber: Shade anything you partly agree/disagree with in amber.
- Green: Shade the sections you agree with in green.

EXTRACT

From Amity Shlaes, The Forgotten Man: A New History of the Great Depression, *published in 2007.*

Roosevelt's errors... were devastating. He created regulatory aid and relief agencies based on the premise that recovery could be achieved only through a large military-style effort. Some of these were useful – the financial institutions he established on entering office. Some were inspiring – the Civilian Conservation Corps for example which created parks, bridges and roads we still enjoy today... CCC workers planted a total of 3 billion trees across the country. Establishing the Securities and Exchange Commission, enacting banking reform – as well as the reform of the Federal Reserve system – all had a stabilising effect...

Other new institutions such as the National Recovery Administration, did damage... NRA rules were so stringent they perversely hurt businesses. They frightened away capital and they discouraged employers from hiring workers.

Roosevelt's later New Deals, 1935–39

The Second New Deal, 1935–38

In 1935 Roosevelt introduced a second New Deal which was more radical than the first in many ways, particularly in terms of favouring the poorer classes over the rich.

The reasons for the Second New Deal

Roosevelt needed to respond to the demands of his more radical supporters lest they oppose him:

- Congress itself demanded radical measures and Roosevelt did not want to lose the initiative: he wanted to introduce his own legislation rather than rubber-stamping that introduced by Congress.
- He was increasingly frustrated by the wealthy classes and big business who opposed him despite the New Deal having saved the system of capitalism.
- He wanted to appeal to the less advantaged ranks in society whom he believed had been forgotten in the past.

While the Second New Deal appeared wide-ranging, Roosevelt was still conservative in many measures; for example, in May 1935 he warned about spending public funds wastefully. We should not over-exaggerate the radicalism of the legislation.

Second New Deal legislation
Emergency Relief Appropriation Act, 1935

This measure comprised the biggest expenditure in US history at that time for relief, with $45.5 billion being earmarked for public works schemes. It set up the following:

- The Works Progress Administration (WPA), which had employed 20 per cent of the workforce by 1940 on a variety of schemes. Two of its large-scale projects were Fort Knox, the repository of US gold reserves, and the Lincoln Tunnel in New York.
- The National Youth Administration (NYA) to provide part-time jobs for students so they could complete their educational studies.

Rural Electrification Act, 1935

This was formed to provide electricity to rural areas where it may not have been profitable for private companies to do so. The REA offered loans at low rates of interest to farmers to form co-operatives to provide electricity. By 1941, 35 per cent of farms had electricity: 773 systems with 348,000 miles of transmission lines had been built in six years.

The Revenue Act, 1935

This was often known as the 'Soak the Rich' Act. It increased taxes to pay for New Deal reforms, for example increasing the maximum tax on incomes over $50,000 from 50 to 75 per cent. While the increased taxes raised comparatively little, as only 1 per cent of the population earned salaries of over $10,000, it was the principle which detractors objected to.

Social Security Act, 1935

This was the first extensive measure of social security available to all who qualified. It instituted old age pensions and disability pensions, which, although meagre, set a precedent for future development. Unemployment benefit of $18 per week was offered for a limited period of 16 weeks.

The Act was a major break with federal government tradition of not getting involved in welfare.

- It did, however, have to be self-financing. Recipients of old age pensions had to pay into the system and the amount they received depended on how much they paid.
- There were also significant omissions including domestic and agricultural workers who earned too little to contribute. Healthcare insurance was not included due to the opposition of the powerful American Medical Association which would not accept any constraint on its right to decide what fees to charge patients.

Wagner (National Labour Relations) Act, 1937

For the first time, trade unions were given legal rights such as that of collective bargaining, and a three-man National Labour Relations Board was set up to ensure fair play between employers and their workforce in disputes. The Wagner Act was initiated in Congress but supported by Roosevelt.

Labour unions in the USA

Employers in the USA had a tradition of hostility to trade unions and many had adopted 'Yellow Dog' clauses which prevented their employees from joining them. The National Recovery Act outlawed these clauses and set up a Labour Board to facilitate the right of workers to join unions. However, many employers ignored this. **Henry Ford** even employed strong-arm men to intimidate workers, deterring them from joining a union or becoming involved in disputes.

! Simple essay style

Below is a sample A-level exam question. Use your own knowledge and the information on the opposite page to produce a plan for this question. Choose four general points, and provide three pieces of specific information to support each general point.

Once you have planned your essay, write the introduction and conclusion for the essay. The introduction should list the points to be discussed in the essay. The conclusion should summarise the key points and justify which point was the most important.

The Second New Deal was more radical than the first.' Assess the validity of this statement in respect of the increased role of federal government.

i Turning assertion into argument   a

Below are a series of definitions, a sample essay title and two sample conclusions. One of the conclusions achieves a high mark because it contains an argument. The other achieves a lower mark because it contains only description and assertion. Identify which is which. The mark scheme on page 7 will help you.

- **Description**: a detailed account.
- **Assertion**: a statement of fact or an opinion which is not supported by a reason.
- **Reason**: a statement which explains or justifies something.
- **Argument**: an assertion justified with a reason.

'The Second New Deal represented a huge increase in the role of federal government.' How far do you agree with this statement?

Student 1

The Second New Deal marked a major change in the role of government. As a result the role of government grew far more extensive. It affected people in ways no government had ever done before. Of course there was a lot of opposition to this. This is not to suggest that all the legislation was especially effective. Some had limited impact. Nevertheless even this marked precedents for future development. At the end of the period of the Second New Deal, the role of government was transformed. However, we should not over-exaggerate its radical nature: Roosevelt remained a fiscal conservative and warned in May 1935 of the folly of government overspending. Basically Roosevelt saw the scale of the Depression and developed the role of government to address this.

Student 2

The Second New Deal saw to a large degree a huge increase in the role of government. However, one should not exaggerate this. Roosevelt personally remained a fiscal conservative who sought to balance the budget, and still saw many of the measures passed as temporary until prosperity returned. In May 1935, for example, he warned of the dangers of government wastefulness. Many of the measures were based on loans, such as the Rural Electrification Administration which lent money to farmers to provide electricity. Others were temporary, as exemplified by the word 'Emergency' in their title – for example, the Emergency Relief Appropriation Act of 1935 which allocated $45.5 billion for public works schemes to provide temporary employment and kick-start the economy. Even the Revenue Act of 1935 which raised taxes for the wealthy was intended in part to reduce the need for government deficit spending. Clearly, however, many of the measures did set precedents for increased government activity – for example, the social Security Act, which introduced nationwide pensions and unemployment benefits for the first time.

Conflict of ideas over the role of federal government

The New Deal attracted much opposition, from the right because it was too radical and the left because it wasn't radical enough.

The right

Many of the businessmen who had supported Roosevelt's measures when capitalism seemed threatened with collapse now opposed them when it appeared to be saved. In particular, they resented the high taxes to pay for New Deal programmes.

Liberty Leaguers

The Liberty League was formed in April 1934 by conservative Democrats and Republicans to oppose the New Deal. They believed the free market unregulated by government was the best means of ensuring lasting economic recovery. By 1936 the League had 125,000 members – although most of these fell away after Roosevelt's 1936 electoral victory.

The left

Roosevelt was afraid that left-wing groups would merge to form a large new political party to oppose him in the 1936 election.

'Share Our Wealth'

'Share Our Wealth' was a scheme designed to end poverty, advocated by popular Louisiana Senator **Huey Long**. Long proposed that:

- all private fortunes over $3 million should be confiscated and the money redistributed
- the government should fund pensions and introduce a minimum wage
- every family should be guaranteed an income of $2,000–3,000 per year.

Roosevelt feared Long would stand against him in the 1936 presidential election. However, Long was assassinated in September 1935 and 'Share Our Wealth' ceased to be influential.

Thunder on the Left

Political groups favouring more radical measures were known as 'Thunder on the Left', advocating policies such as **nationalisation of public utilities** and using empty factories to provide jobs for the unemployed. Leaders included Governor Floyd B. Olson of Minnesota until his death in 1936 and the brothers Robert Jnr and Philip Lafayette.

Opposition to the Second New Deal

Roosevelt faced significant opposition to the Second New Deal made worse as problems emerged in his second term of office. His first major battle was with the Supreme Court.

The Supreme Court

One main task of the Supreme Court is to ensure that legislation is constitutional, or whether the framers have the powers actually to make the laws they envisage. As the New Deal developed in the mid-1930s, the Supreme Court increasingly declared legislation unconstitutional. On 'Black Monday' 27 May 1935, the Supreme Court found several pieces of New Deal legislation unconstitutional including the NIRA, and, in January 1936, the AAA.

The Judiciary Reform Bill

Roosevelt's response was to reform the Supreme Court to make it more amenable. In February 1936 the Judiciary Reform Bill proposed to:

- raise the number of Supreme Court judges from nine to 15
- replace existing judges by a presidential appointee when they became 70 years of age.

Roosevelt's aim was to appoint more judges who would support him. However, the Senate saw that this was an attempt to control the Supreme Court and rejected the bill by 70 votes to 20.

Roosevelt had been defeated, although, recognising his huge electoral victory in the 1936 presidential election, the Supreme Court did become less obstructive.

Opposition of the wealthy and conservatives

Roosevelt continued to face opposition from big business and the wealthy. However, Republicans were increasingly joined by more conservative Democrats who thought Roosevelt was becoming too powerful. Indeed opponents in Congress issued a Conservative Manifesto in December 1937 calling for lower taxes and more restrictions on industrial action.

Mid-term congressional elections, 1938

Roosevelt openly supported liberal- as opposed to conservative-minded Democrats in the mid-term elections in 1938. This caused problems in establishing working relations with the new Congress when it met.

! Develop the detail

Below are a sample essay title and a paragraph written in answer to this question. The paragraph contains a limited amount of detail. Annotate the paragraph to add additional detail to the answer.

'The strength of the opposition to the New Deals posed a real threat to its successful implementation.' Assess the validity of this statement.

> The New Deal attracted opposition from the left and the right. Many on the right formed the Liberty League but it wasn't very effective. Huey Long was a powerful opponent on the left with his 'Share Our Wealth' programme. However the biggest threat came from the Supreme Court.

! How far do you agree?

Read the extract below and summarise each of its arguments. Use your knowledge to agree or contradict.

Arguments in extract	Knowledge that corroborates	Knowledge that contradicts
1		
2		
3		

EXTRACT A

From Richard Hofstadter, The Age of Reform, *published in 1968.*

Students of the Court fight are fond of remarking that Roosevelt won his case, because the direction of the Court's decisions began to change while the fight was in progress and because Justice Van Devanter's retirement enabled the president to appoint a liberal justice and decisively change the composition of the Court. It seems important, however, to point out that a very heavy price had to be paid for even this pragmatic attempt to alter a great and sacrosanct conservative institution. The Court fight alienated many principled liberals and enabled many of FDR's conservative opponents to portray him to the public more convincingly as a man who aspired to personal dictatorship and aimed at the subversion of the Republic.

The economy

Boom to bust and recovery

The economy boomed in the 1920s before overheating in the later years of the decade to usher in the Great Depression from 1929. The New Deal only partly helped recovery.

While the economy seemed prosperous during the 1920s (see page 52), there were warning signs.

Overproduction

The economic boom was dependent on continuous production, which was in turn dependent on continuous demand. However, by the late 1920s demand was falling as more goods were produced than could be sold. One survey in 1929 estimated that incomes of 80 per cent of Americans were so low that they lived close to **subsistence** even when they were in work.

The bull market

During the late 1920s demand for shares grew considerably. This created a condition known as the **bull market**. Demand for shares was based on the assumption that share prices would continue to rise. Many bought shares on credit – 10 per cent deposit and the remainder on weekly payments – known as 'buying on the margin'. However, if the boom collapsed they would be left with valueless shares they still had to continue paying for at the price of their original investment.

The Wall Street Crash

In October 1929 the Wall Street stock market crashed. On 29 October, 16,410,030 shares were sold as their price collapsed: by mid-November $30 billion had been lost. This event led to the Depression as economic confidence was destroyed. It was a key indicator of how precarious the economy was.

Structural weaknesses

There were various structural weaknesses in the management of the US economy which left it prone to failures.

Banking

The banking system was outmoded:
- The Federal Reserve Banks (see page 34) operated in their own interests rather than those of the nation as a whole.

- National banks were regulated by the federal system. However, there were also 30,000 relatively small local banks which remained completely outside the Reserve Bank system. In some cases they issued their own currencies which would only be accepted in their local areas, and were completely unprotected against collapse.

In order to keep the economy buoyant, the Federal Reserve system favoured low interest rates. But this fuelled the easy credit and increasing amounts of debt to which many were subject.

Stock market

The stock market was also relatively unregulated so unscrupulous brokers could speculate and involve themselves in insider dealing to make prices rise and fall artificially (see above).

Government

The reluctance of federal government to regulate the economy left business interests relatively free to behave unscrupulously (see pages 52).

The impact of the New Deals and War on economic recovery

The New Deal

The New Deals did little to improve the economy. For example, the national total of personal income was $86 billion in 1929, falling to $73 billion ten years later. Unemployment had fallen from 13 million in 1933 to 9 million in 1939, but this was still a huge figure. When Roosevelt had reduced expenditure in 1937 the result was the 'Roosevelt recession', which suggested there had been no real lasting economic improvement. Unemployment between 1937 and 1938 rose from 7 million to over 10 million and national income fell by 13 per cent within a year.

The Second World War

The Second World War substantially aided economic recovery and masked the failures of the New Deal. By 1942 the USA achieved full employment. After this there were labour shortages. During the war years, the USA produced more war materiel than all its enemies added together. Farm income grew by 250 per cent.

Eliminate irrelevance

a

Below are a sample exam question and a paragraph written in answer to this question. Read the paragraph and identify the parts that are not directly relevant to the question. Draw a line through the information that is irrelevant and justify your deletions in the margin.

'It was the impact of the Second World War rather than the New Deal which brought economic prosperity back to the USA.' Assess the validity of this statement.

The New Deal itself did little to improve the economy. The national total of personal income for example fell from $86 billion in 1929, to $73 billion in 1939. Although unemployment had reduced from 13 million in 1933 to 9 million in 1939, this was still a huge figure. When Roosevelt reduced expenditure in 1937 the result was the Roosevelt recession, which suggested there had been no real lasting economic improvement. This resulted in growing opposition to Roosevelt's policies as shown by the mid-term congressional elections of 1938, which saw large gains for conservative Democrats and Republicans. Roosevelt had once said that everyone was against him but the electorate, but this no longer seemed to be the case.

The Second World War, however, substantially aided economic recovery and masked the failures of the New Deal. By 1942 the USA achieved full employment. After this there were labour shortages. Unlike in the First World War, women were widely recruited to make up the shortages: 6.5 million women were in the workforce by 1944. During the war years, the USA produced more war materiel than all its enemies added together. Farm income grew by 250 per cent. Between 1941 and 1945 the USA produced 86,000 tanks, 290,000 aircraft and 15 million rifles.

How far do you agree?

Read the following extract and summarise each of its arguments. Use your knowledge to agree or contradict.

Arguments in extract	Knowledge that corroborates	Knowledge that contradicts
1		
2		
3		

EXTRACT

From Paul Johnson, A History of the American People, *published in 1997.*

Another myth that has grown up about these times is that the twenties Boom was a mere drunken spending spree, bound to end in disaster, and that beneath a veneer of prosperity was an abyss of poverty. That is not true. The prosperity was very widespread. It was not universal; in the farming community it was patchy, and it largely excluded certain older industrial communities such as the New England textile trade. But growth was spectacular. On a 1933–38 index of 100, it was 58 in 1921 and 110 in 1929. This involved an increase in national income from $59.4 to $87.2 billion in eight years, with real per capita income rising from $522 to $716: not Babylonian luxury but a modest comfort never thitherto thought possible.

The heart of the consumer boom was in personal transport, which in a vast country, where some of the new cities were already 30 miles across, was not a luxury. At the beginning of 1914, 1,258,062 cars were registered in the US, which produced 569,054 during the year. Production rose to 5,621,715 in 1929, by which time cars registered in the US totalled 26,501,443, five-sixths of the world's production...

Social and cultural developments

'The Jazz Age' in the 1920s

During the 1920s there were significant changes in US culture, from a growing interest in jazz music and less restrained dancing to greater liberation for women. However, one should not over-exaggerate these: most people retained conservative values and distrusted the new trends.

Jazz was the defining sound of US cities in the 1920s. It was rooted in black American musical traditions. In the 1920s jazz became more mainstream, as performed by musicians such as Louis Armstrong, providing the rhythms for new dance crazes such as the Charleston and Black Bottom. In America's cities, nightclubs attracted young people, especially '**flappers**', while jazz music could be heard in the home for the first time through radio and records. Many older people felt jazz encouraged immorality in the young, particularly as it had its origins in black American culture.

New social values and the role of women

On the surface, the period of the 1920s offered new opportunities to women, particularly in the workplace and in social life. However, while employment opportunities arose, few women enjoyed managerial positions, and long-term aspirations widely focused on marriage and childcare. The media made much of 'flappers' – liberated young women who enjoyed dancing and nightclubs and wore skimpy clothes – but these were very much a part of city life and for most it was simply a phase before settling down to family life.

Politics

Women enjoyed limited political opportunities. Although the Nineteenth Amendment of 1920 gave them the right to vote, their political voice was muted. There were few women in political office – 145 in all the various state legislatures in 1928, only 2 out of 435 delegates in the House of Representatives and no female Senators.

Employment

Some women found success in the film industry and fashion, although the numbers were small. Women found plentiful employment in office work as clerks and typists. However, it was rare for them to move up to managerial positions, and, for those who did, it was often at the sacrifice of marriage and family.

Women's rights

Women were increasingly concerned with issues such as birth control and healthcare championed by the American Birth Control League, but largely found government and conservative voices unsympathetic. One of the few measures aimed at women was the 1921 Sheppard–Towner Act which gave states federal aid to develop healthcare for pregnant women. However, many feminists believed this simply reinforced the role of women as child-bearers and detracted from the need for birth control.

The failure of Prohibition and its significance

In 1919 the Eighteenth Amendment banned the sale, transportation and manufacture of intoxicating liquor within the USA in order to end consumption of alcohol. This was Prohibition. It was widely supported in rural and small-town USA, by conservative and religious groups, but was generally a failure. It ended in 1933.

Reasons for Prohibition

Prohibition was supported by a wide variety of interest groups:
- Many women's groups argued that alcohol consumption was a means by which men oppressed them.
- Big business owners claimed that drunkenness was a cause of dangers and inefficiency in the workplace.
- Many religious groups believed that alcohol was a cause of immoral behaviour.

In addition, many breweries were owned by German-Americans, and it was felt to be unpatriotic to be drinking their products when the USA was at war with Germany.

Why Prohibition failed

Prohibition failed to achieve the results that its supporters had expected:
- It was impossible to police the 18,700 miles of US coastline, making it easy to smuggle in alcohol from ships.
- Bootleggers manufactured and distributed alcohol illegally.
- Alcohol for industrial purposes was legal so it was easy to divert this into alcoholic drinks.
- Treasury agents charged with the enforcement of prohibition were poorly resourced and paid.

It was estimated that less than 5 per cent of illegal alcohol was intercepted, while the profits from the illicit industry were $2 billion per year.

Quick quizzes at **www.hoddereducation.co.uk/myrevisionnotes**

Below is an extract to read. You are asked to summarise the interpretation about the failures of prohibition, and then develop a counter-argument.

Interpretation offered by the extract:

_____

_____

Counter-argument:

_____

_____

EXTRACT

Extract from Bill Bryson, One Summer: America 1927, _published in 2013._

Almost everything about Prohibition was inept or farcical. The Treasury was charged with enforcing the laws, but it wholly lacked the necessary qualifications, funding or zeal for the job. Starved of resources by Congress, the Prohibition Department hired just 1520 agents and gave them the impossible task of trying to stop the production and consumption of alcohol among 100 million citizens (or about 75,000 people per agent) within an area of 3.5 million square miles while simultaneously protecting 18,700 miles of coastline and border from smugglers. The federal government expected the states to take up the slack and enforce the laws, but the states were almost everywhere disinclined to do so. By 1927 the average state was spending eight times more on enforcing fish and game laws than it spent on Prohibition.

The economic cost to the nation was enormous. The federal government lost $500 million a year on liquor taxes – nearly a tenth of national income. At state level the pain was even greater. New York before prohibition relied on liquor taxes for half its income. It is little wonder that states were reluctant to find the money in their reduced budgets to prosecute a law that was impoverishing them.

i **Develop the detail**

Below are a sample essay title and a paragraph written in answer to this question. The paragraph contains a limited amount of detail. Annotate the paragraph to add additional detail to the answer.

To what extent did the role and status of women change during the 1920s?

The role and status of women changed little during the 1920s. More women found employment but it tended to be low-skilled. Their role in politics was very limited. Women's issues in the public eye tended to relate to child and healthcare. Although the media in particular showed more women as liberated, in reality their lives were little different from earlier decades.

Social impact of the Depression and the Second World War REVISED

The Depression of the 1930s and Second World War had a considerable social impact on Americans.

Social impact of the Depression

Effects on workers, families and farmers

The human cost of the Depression was enormous. The USA lacked an infrastructure to deal with mass employment. There was for example no federal aid and charities could not cope. The prevailing philosophy had previously been that the unemployed were to blame for their plight and they could find work with determination and effort. While the Depression showed that this was not the case, there were few ideas to replace it.

The extent of relief

Before 1932 no state had any recognised system of unemployment insurance and only 11 operated any form of pension scheme. There were few private pension schemes and they catered for the relatively well-off.

Workers

The only alternative for many people facing unemployment was to sell all their possessions and then rely on charities who were under tremendous pressures as the demands on them grew as their funds dried up. Many unemployed became **hobos** moving across the country in search of work – by 1932 it was estimated that there were over 1 million itinerant workers without regular or fixed employment.

Families

The strain on families led to a fall in marriages, from 1.23 million in 1929 to 982,000 by 1932, with a concomitant fall in the birth rate. Suicide rates increased from 14 per 10,000 in 1929 to 17.4 by 1932 – and the majority of elderly people with few support mechanisms were living below the poverty line.

Social impact of the Second World War

The Second World War had a major effect on people's lives in the USA.

Migration to urban and rural centres

It is estimated that 27 million Americans moved during the war, while the population of rural areas fell by 29 per cent. Most moved to areas with defence plants, notably California whose population rose by 72 per cent during the war years, and 200,000 moved to government employment in Washington DC. Throughout the USA there were huge housing shortages: one solution was to build barrack-style accommodation which at one time housed 1.5 million people. In 1943, partially as a result of competition for housing, there were severe race riots in Detroit which left 34 dead.

Role and status of women

The war significantly affected the role and status of women:
- Many faced huge problems having to juggle childcare with long working hours.
- There was in particular a shortage of housing in urban areas and many families faced overcrowded conditions.
- Women also faced shortages of materials deployed for the war effort. They grew their own produce in 'Victory gardens', joined the Women's Land Army to replace male agricultural workers, and learned to manage without luxuries.
- To accommodate the growing numbers of women in the workforce the Community Facilities Act of 1941 provided childcare facilities for women in defence plants. However, the demand far exceeded the supply.

Numbers of women workers:

Year	Total	% of women in the manufacturing workforce
1941	14,600,000	22
1944	19,370,000	32

Dislocation

The demands of wartime inevitably led to considerable dislocation, with 15 million serving in the military, many overseas. Their absence led to a growth in the divorce rate, and youth crime. However, the population increased, notably in the **'furlough babies'** conceived during periods of leave.

Quick quizzes at **www.hoddereducation.co.uk/myrevisionnotes**

Spectrum of importance

Below are a sample exam question and a list of general points which could be used to answer the question. Use your own knowledge and the information on the opposite page to reach a judgement about the importance of these general points to the question posed. Write numbers on the spectrum below to indicate their relative importance. Having done this, write a brief justification of your placement, explaining why some of these factors are more important than others. The resulting diagram could form the basis of an essay plan.

How far were people's lives transformed by the Great Depression and impact of the Second World War in the USA?

1 Impact of unemployment

2 Effects on Depression on family life

3 Hobos

4 Migration during the Second World War

5 The impact of the war on women

6 Social dislocation during the war years

Least important ←――――――――――――――――――――――――――――――→ Most important

Introducing and concluding an argument

Look at the key points of the answer.

1 How good is the proposed introduction?

2 Could it be improved – especially in relation to Level 5 answers? Write a conclusion for this answer.

'The Depression had a greater impact on people's lives than the home front in the Second World War.' Assess the validity of this statement.

Key points

- Human cost of the Depression
- Little state relief and charities unable to cope with demand
- Strain on families, e.g. growth in divorce and suicide rates
- Scale of internal migration in the Second World War
- Growth in numbers of women in work
- Social dislocation increase in divorce rates and youth crime

Introduction

Both the Depression and the impact of the Second World War on the USA had a significant effect on people's lives, although they affected them in different ways. The Depression for example saw massive unemployment, with most effects emanating from that. The Second World War on the other hand saw a huge growth in employment opportunities especially in war work, and a massive migration to centres of this employment – as many as 27 million people may have moved locations during the war years. Both the Depression and war caused dislocation, however – both saw the divorce rate grow, for example. However, I hope to argue in this essay that in the long term the social impact of the war was in fact greater than that of the Depression because it was more permanent for many people affected by it.

Social, regional and ethnic divisions

The period 1920 to 1941 was marked by social, regional and ethnic divisions often occasioned by conflict between traditional values and new trends, particularly those taking place in cities.

Countryside versus city

While 1920 saw for the first time a majority of Americans living in urban centres, most of these were still comparatively small and clung to conservative values. These included hard work, thrift and moral values driven by deeply held religious beliefs. Many saw larger cities as hotbeds of immorality, as exemplified by nightclubs, dancing and illegal drinking of alcohol.

- Cities were also seen as centres of crime fuelled by the provision of 'bootleg' liquor.
- Cities were seen as centres of revolutionary ideas such as communism introduced by the 'new immigrants'.

The widespread rural support for Republican politics in the 1920s could be seen in part as a desire to turn back the clock.

Perceived tensions between countryside and city life

Countryside	City
Traditional conservative values	New ideas
Moral lifestyles	Immorality and hedonism
Deeply religious	Irreligious
Peaceful and orderly	Crime-ridden and violent
Hard-working	Indolent

Clearly these tensions were exaggerated and imprecise: most city dwellers were equally as hard-working, thrifty and religious as their rural counterparts, while crime and violence happened equally in rural areas. However, many perceived them at the time to be accurate.

Divisions between the North, West and South

Divisions between North, West and South continued, with the North perceived as the centre of big business which dominated politics.

- The differences in wealth were real enough, however: in 1929 per capita income in the North was $921 and in the South-East $365.
- New industries such as car manufacture were also drawn to the North and Mid-West because of the well-established communications networks, the proximity to large centres of population and a mobile workforce.

- On the other hand the development of synthetic fibres and reductions in the amount of material needed in changing female fashions reduced the need for cottons grown and manufactured in the South.

African-Americans and the rise of the Ku Klux Klan

African-Americans continued to face discrimination both in the South and North. However, they were faced in the 1920s by a resurgent Ku Klux Klan.

The Klan re-emerged as a potent force in the South and Mid-West during the 1920s: it had an estimated 100,000 followers by 1921.

Beliefs and methods

The Ku Klux Klan advocated white supremacy and attacked blacks, Jews, Catholics and any it felt were supporting unAmerican ideas. It opposed what it considered as foreign or immoral influences such as jazz music.

The Klan held rallies and marches to demonstrate their presence, and practised acts of brutality in particular against African-Americans whom they terrorised to keep at the lowest strata of society.

Influence

During its peak of popularity, the Klan could control both politicians and police in certain areas. It is alleged that in 1924 it helped elect governors in Maine, Ohio, Colorado and Louisiana. Nevertheless they had little influence in bigger cities where many people may have been more sophisticated in their views.

The Klan did, however, maintain a national profile, for example through large-scale parades in big cities: over 50,000 marched through Washington DC on 13 September 1926. At its peak in 1924, the Klan may have had as many as 4 million members.

However, the Klan lost support when rocked with allegations of corruption and scandals, including the rape of a secretary by Indiana Klan leader David Stephenson; by 1929 its membership had fallen to 20,000.

Impact on black Americans

While the Klan succeeded in terrorising many black Americans, it also stimulated the migration north to industrial cities (see page 40), and encouraged many to sympathise with and where possible join separatist organisations such as Marcus Garvey's Universal Negro Improvement Society which advocated black people should return to Africa.

! RAG – rate the timeline · a

Below are a sample essay question and a timeline. Read the question, study the timeline and, using three coloured pens, put a Red, Amber or Green star next to the events to show:

- Red: Events and policies that have no relevance to the question.
- Amber: Events and policies that have some significance to the question.
- Green: Events and policies that are directly relevant to the question.

To what extent was the USA marked by social and ethnic divisions in the period 1920 to 1929?

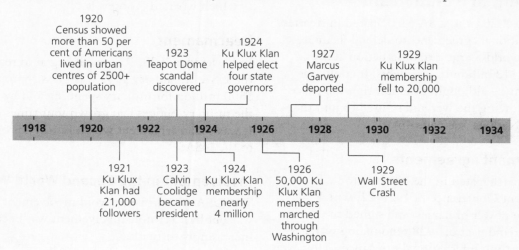

! Summarise the arguments · a

Below are a sample exam question and one of the extracts referred to in the question. You must read the extract and identify the interpretation offered. Look for the arguments of the passage.

With reference to the extract and your contextual knowledge, how convincing do you find the extract in relation to the significance of the Ku Klux Klan in creating social tensions in the USA in the 1920s and 1930s?

Interpretation offered by the extract:

_____

_____

EXTRACT

From Philipp Blom, Fracture: Life and Culture in the West 1918–1938, *published in 2015.*

The Klan's membership was limited to native born white Protestants, and, though its main target of hatred was black Americans, it was also ready to attack anyone suspected of being 'unAmerican', a category that included Jews, Catholics and socialists. The Klan's first leader or 'Imperial Wizard' was William J. Simmonds of Alabama, a former Methodist Episcopal minister suspended by his church for inefficiency...

Though the ensuing decades were to witness a great many Klan-directed attacks on black men and women, including thousands of lynchings, the activities of this second wave KKK were not limited to violence against blacks. The Klansmen began to turn on anyone who did not represent their vision of what it was to be American; they saw themselves as defenders of 'pure womanhood' and guardians of morality, opposing abortion and drinking but also 'loose dancing' and 'roadside parking'. Those accused of violating the Klan's strict moral code were abducted and subjected to a variety of tortures: flogging, branding, tarring and feathering, whipping, mutilation, or in some cases, a cruel and slow death.

The USA and international relations

The USA sought non-involvement in European affairs after the First World War and tried to remain aloof from the Second World War. However, it was too influential and powerful to remain isolated, despite the wishes of many Americans.

The extent of isolationism

During the 1920s, the USA participated in treaties and international agreements to defend its interests. It was the world's largest trading nation and was owed over $12 billion in war debts. It could not be isolationist – although it did not sign the peace treaties following the war and refused to join the League of Nations (see page 46).

Disarmament agreements

The USA participated in the Washington Disarmament Conference of 1921–22, which reduced the power of navies, and signed the Kellogg–Briand pact of 1928 renouncing war as a means of settling international grievances. However, neither of these agreements had sanctions attached.

Good Neighbour

The USA pursued 'Good Neighbour' policies in Latin America – for example, withdrawing troops from the Dominican Republic and Nicaragua in 1924 and encouraging trade; by 1929 the volume of trade with Latin America exceeded $3.2 billion. The policy recognised US economic muscle but seemed less confrontational than earlier in the century (see page 24).

FDR and the end of isolationism

Roosevelt's main foreign policy concern was the rise of the European dictators. The mood in the USA was generally one of strict neutrality, with the USA avoiding being drawn into future conflicts. This was exemplified by a series of Neutrality Acts between 1935 and 1936 in which arms sales to belligerent nations were banned: the fourth in fact banned US citizens to travel on ships of belligerent nations and insisted all goods should be sold on a cash and carry basis.

FDR and the Second World War

Events in the later 1930s escalated to threaten the US stance:
- Full-scale war between Japan and China threatened US interests.
- Germany pursued an expansionist programme which worried Roosevelt.

Rearmament

In December 1938, Roosevelt began to rearm the USA: in January 1939 Congress appropriated $500 million for military spending and by 1941 the military budget had grown four times over. It was this rearmament which restored prosperity to the USA.

Involvement in the Second World War

The USA still strove to avoid involvement in the war but by 1941 non-involvement was becoming increasingly difficult.
- Most Americans wanted the Allies to win, and saw the need to keep them supplied with the materiel to do so. The USA became the 'arsenal of democracy', 'loaning' materiel to Britain under the 'Lend-Lease' agreement. However, by 1941 there was an undeclared naval war in the Atlantic as German U-boats targeted all ships en route for Britain (and from June 1941 the USSR), including US ones.
- The USA was boycotting crucial supplies to Japan, including oil. The Japanese were becoming increasingly desperate to secure new oil supplies, capturing the Dutch East Indies where there were plentiful supplies, for example. This involved destroying the US fleet in the Pacific so they couldn't prevent this.

When Japan attacked the US fleet at Pearl Harbor on 7 December 1941, the USA declared war. Japan's ally, Nazi Germany, declared war on the USA on 11 December. The USA was now a full participant in the Second World War.

Comparing interpretations

Below is an A-level style question. Read the three extracts that follow and then plan an answer for each of them.

> Using your understanding of the historical context, assess how convincing the arguments in these extracts are in relation to American foreign policy in the years 1920 to 1941.

EXTRACT A

From Harold Evans, The American Century, *published in 1999.*

On 6 April 1927, the tenth anniversary of America's entry into world war, France's Foreign Minister Aristide Briand exported the 'spirit of Locarno' [reference to a treaty made between European nations in 1925, settling their differences] by proposing a French–American pact of peace. Coolidge and his peppery new Secretary of State, Frank B. Kellogg, shied away from tying the US to France, but American public opinion loved the idea that war could be banished by proclamation. In a neat manoeuvre, the administration made the pact multilateral – and meaningless.

The Kellogg–Briand pact outlawing war, with endless qualifications, passed the Senate 85–1 in January 1929. Nearly every country signed but the unrecognised Soviet Union was excluded and the pact had no teeth. It simply buttressed America's illusion that with a few moral gestures it could wash its hands of world affairs. When Coolidge came to sign the pact, his pen ran out of ink.

EXTRACT B

From Oliver Stone and Peter Kuznick, The Untold History of the United States, *published in 2013.*

World peace, however noble, was no more the capitalists' primary concern than was achieving wealth and power through a competitive marketplace. Through a dizzying array of formal and informal business agreements, a network of multinational companies based in the United States, England and Germany colluded to capture markets and control prices... Typical of these arrangements, Edsel Ford sat on the board of the German chemical firm IB Farben's US subsidiary, General Aniline and Film, while Farben general manager Carl Bosch sat on the board of Ford's European subsidiary. Similar arrangements tied together Farben, Du Pont, GM, Standard Oil and Chase Bank...

Henry Ford... attested to Hitler's pacific intentions. On 28 August 1939, just four days prior to the invasion of Poland, Ford assured the *Boston Globe* that Hitler was just bluffing. The Germans 'don't dare have a war and they know it,' he said. A week later, after the German invasion had begun, he had the temerity to remark to a friend, 'there hasn't been a shot fired. The whole thing has just been made up by Jew bankers.'

EXTRACT C

From Roger Thompson, The Golden Door, *published in 1969.*

Americans led by such men as Senators Borah and Wheeler or 'The Lone Eagle', Charles Lindbergh, refused to accept the implications and responsibilities of world power, or to acknowledge that in the twentieth century no great nation is an island entire unto itself, economically or diplomatically. The famous neutrality legislation of New Deal days (1935, 1936, 1937) which forbade the export of arms or loans to belligerents, or Americans to travel on belligerents' ships, was a futile attempt to turn the self-righteous back on a street-full of armed men. As dictators marched, Americans legislated.

When in September 1939, Britain and France declared war on Hitler, America was waking from twenty years of nostalgic dreaming. In 1938 provision was made by Congress for the construction of a two ocean navy (Atlantic and Pacific) by an appropriation of $1 billion. Two years later the president called for the building of 50,000 planes a year and limited conscription. But Roosevelt had to tread warily, for isolationist feeling, as propagated by the 'America First' movement... was vociferous and influential.

Recommended reading

- Piers Brendon, *The Dark Valley: A Panorama of the 1930s* (2001), Chapters iv, xi and xx
- Hugh Brogan, *The Penguin History of the United States* (1985), Chapters 22 and 23
- Lucy Moore, *Anything Goes* (2008)
- Amity Shlaes, *The Forgotten Man: A New History of the Great Depression* (2009)

Exam focus (A-level)

Below is a sample essay. It was written in response to an A-level question. Read it and the comments around it.

'The period 1920 to 1945 saw deep tensions in society in the USA.' Assess the validity of this view.

The period 1920 to 1945 was marked by deep tensions in society caused by factors such as perceived threats to traditional values and morality, the onset of economic depression in the early 1930s, and the impact of the Second World War. Often these tensions are exemplified by social, regional and ethnic divisions, particularly those taking place in cities.

> Introduction sets out question parameters and signposts how it will be answered.

The 1920 census saw most Americans living in urban centres for the first time. However, most of these remained small settlements and clung to the traditional, conservative values associated with the countryside. There was widespread distrust of larger cities which were believed to be centres of immorality, illicit drinking and shameful behaviour. In particular many feared cities were hotbeds of racial mixing, crime and radical political ideas. Much of this focused on racism, where for example 'new immigrants' were accused of introducing 'unAmerican' ideas such as communism, and African-Americans of seducing white girls with music and dancing.

> Exemplifies fears which led to tensions.

Clearly these tensions were exaggerated and imprecise: most city dwellers were just as hard-working, thrifty and religious as their rural counterparts, while crime and violence happened equally in rural areas. However, many perceived them at the time to be accurate. One response was the widespread rural support for Republican politics in the 1920s which could be seen in part as a desire to turn back the clock to more traditional values of the previous century.

> Emphasises the perceived threat rather than the reality.

However, these tensions also manifested themselves in more invidious ways such as support of the Ku Klux Klan, which re-emerged as a potent force in the South and Mid-West during the 1920s: it had an estimated 100,000 followers by 1921. During the peak of popularity, the Klan could control both politicians and police in certain areas. It is alleged that in 1924 it helped elect governors in Maine, Ohio, Colorado and Louisiana. Nevertheless it had little influence in bigger cities where many people were more sophisticated in their views and dismissive of simplistic solutions to social issues, illustrating again the tensions between urban and more rural areas.

> Returns to question focus.

While the Klan succeeded in terrorising many black Americans, it also stimulated the migration north to industrial cities and encouraged many to sympathise with and where possible join separatist organisations such as Marcus Garvey's Universal Negro Improvement Society which advocated black people should return to Africa. The 1920s saw tensions between ethnic groups which continued throughout the period under discussion. During the Depression years, black Americans found it more difficult to find work than their white counterparts, while, during the war years, they found plentiful employment but still faced discrimination and racism.

> Follows the issue throughout the period set by the question.

The Depression of the 1930s had a considerable social impact on Americans and encouraged a belief that those who remained wealthy did not care for the suffering of those who did not. The human cost of the Depression was enormous. The USA lacked an infrastructure to deal with mass employment. There was, for example, no federal

Quick quizzes at **www.hoddereducation.co.uk/myrevisionnotes**

aid and charities could not cope. The prevailing philosophy had previously been that the unemployed were to blame for their plight and they could find work with determination and effort. Ironically those who migrated in search of work faced hostility from more prosperous areas such as California. Many unemployed indeed became hobos moving across the country in search of work – by 1932 it was estimated that there were over 1 million itinerant workers without regular or fixed employment.

Exemplifies contradictions within tensions.

Much of this tension was manifested in support and opposition for Roosevelt and the New Deal. For many poorer people, Roosevelt was a saviour. He won a huge majority in the 1936 presidential election. However, many of the wealthy saw him as a traitor to his class. Many of the businessmen who had supported Roosevelt's measures when capitalism seemed threatened with collapse now opposed them when it appeared to be saved. In particular, they resented the high taxes to pay for New Deal programmes.

The Second World War had a major effect on people's lives in the USA but exacerbated existing tensions. It is estimated that 27 million Americans moved during the war, while the population of rural areas fell by 29 per cent. Most moved to areas with defence plants, notably California whose population rose by 72 per cent during the war years, and 200,000 moved to government employment in Washington DC. Throughout the USA there were huge housing shortages: one solution was to build barrack-style accommodation which at one time housed 1.5 million people. Housing shortages, along with continuing discrimination, were in part responsible for the severe 1943 race riots in Detroit.

The demands of wartime inevitably led to considerable dislocation, with 15 million serving in the military, many overseas. Their absence led to a growth in the divorce rate, and youth crime. Many women gained in confidence through juggling long working hours with childcare and domestic responsibilities: this was to lead to a greater assertiveness when their menfolk returned in 1945.

It will be seen then that the period 1920 to 1945 saw considerable tensions in society in the USA. Some were the result of new phenomena such as the impact of the Second World War, while others predated the period such as the development of cities, with perceived immorality, radical political ideas and ways of life which seemed to threaten traditional values. The tensions were commonly between traditional ideas as exemplified by rural conservatism, and new approaches often initiated by the entry of foreign and black American influences into the cities. In this context, developments such as the onset of Depression and involvement in the Second World War simply exacerbated tensions which already existed, while causing new ones such as, in the case of the former, mass unemployment, and, with the latter, severe housing shortages. Often these tensions were based on ethnic or geographical divisions. Whether the perceived causes were real or not however, the tensions themselves were acutely felt.

Conclusion is summarising issues discussed.

Valid judgement supported by issues discussed within the essay.

This is a confident, well-structured response, with arguments clearly expressed. There is sufficient analysis of key features with valid supporting knowledge to warrant Level 5. The overall judgement is based on relevant criteria.

Reverse engineering (AO1)

The best essays are based on careful plans. Read the essay and the examiner's comments and try to work out the general points of the plan used to write the essay. Once you have done this, note down the specific examples used to support each general point.

Domestic politics, 1945–60

The USA enjoyed unparalleled prosperity during the years 1945 to 1960, but this did not preclude tensions in domestic politics, particularly during the Truman years 1945 to 1952.

Truman and post-war reconstruction

Harry S. Truman was vice president at the time of President Roosevelt's death in April 1945 and largely followed his plans for post-war reconstruction.

Economic Bill of Rights, 1944

The reality was, in fact, that post-war prosperity was such that legislation to promote employment appeared unnecessary. The USA maintained full employment. However, it faced severe problems in terms of labour relations.

Labour relations

The post-war period saw considerable inflation – a 25 per cent rise in food prices between 1945 and 1947 – while wartime restrictions on wage rises were slow to be repealed. This led to a period of considerable industrial unrest, particularly in 1946:

- General Motors employees demanded wage rises of 35 per cent.
- A massive coal strike in April 1946 threatened post-war recovery; most railroads and industrial plants still relied on coal. By May freight loadings had fallen by 75 per cent and many factories had stopped production. The strike was only called off after intense White House intervention.
- Railroad workers threatened industrial action in May; this again was only averted when Truman threatened to draft railroad workers into the armed forces.
- Altogether 6 million workers, or 10 per cent of the labour force, went on strike; at one point during 1946 there were over 5000 separate stoppages.

Taft–Hartley Act, June 1947

Congress passed the Taft–Hartley Act over Truman's veto in June 1947.

- This outlawed union practices such as the closed shop and secondary strikes.
- It made union leaders swear they were non-communist.
- It insisted on an 80-day 'cooling-off' period before strikes could take place; the time would be used to try to agree a settlement.
- It required unions to make annual financial statements available for scrutiny.

Fair Deal

Truman did manage to get some measures passed, which he called the 'Fair Deal'. Most noticeable was an increase in the minimum wage to 75 cents per hour, increased social security benefits and more public sector housing. However, it was small in scope when compared to the range of the New Deal.

The presidency of Eisenhower, 1953–60

Immensely popular as a result of his wartime service as military commander in Europe, **Dwight Eisenhower** was a moderate Republican. His main aim was a balanced budget, which he achieved only three times, notably in 1959 and 1960. He was not, like the Republican presidents of the 1920s, a believer in minimal government and his administration did see various reforms:

- He extended the social security programme.
- He increased the minimum wage from 75 cents to $1.
- In 1953 he created the Department of Health, Education and Welfare to oversee these areas.
- He passed the 1956 Highways Act which saw the construction of 41,000 miles of roads to connect the country: it was the biggest public works scheme in US history to date.

The mid to late 1950s were an age of such unparalleled prosperity that most Americans did not see the need for extensive government legislation, and so Eisenhower's conservative administration matched the prevailing mood.

(!) Use own knowledge to support or contradict   **a**

Below is an extract to read. You are asked to summarise the interpretation about industrial development in the years after the end of the Second World War in the USA, and then develop a counter-argument.

Interpretation offered by the extract:

_____

_____

Counter-argument:

_____

_____

EXTRACT

From Samuel Eliot Morison, The Oxford History of the American People, *published in 1965.*

President Truman did his best to prevent a post-war reaction such as that of the 1920s. In his address of 5 September 1945 to Congress he outlined a 21-point programme of progressive legislation, in accordance with the 'Fair Deal', as he renamed the no longer New Deal. But Congress and the country were in no mood for social experiments. He was also troubled by the attitude of labour. During the war unions had been riding high, and their members made big money out of war-pressured overtime. Once the war was over and industry converted to peacetime production, management did not attempt to reduce wages but cut overtime, and many workers were furious at having their 'take-home' pay thus reduced by as much as 50 per cent. At the same time the cost of living was rising sharply because Congress refused to continue the price controls as Truman requested.

These were the main reasons for strikes, for higher wages in coal, motor cars, steel, electrical appliances and railroads. The coal strike threatened American industry and John L. Lewis, the leader responsible, defied both the president and the courts and got away with it.

(!) RAG – rate the timeline   **a**

Below are a sample exam question and a timeline. Read the question, study the timeline and, using three coloured pens, put a Red, Amber or Green star next to the events to show:

- Red: Events and policies that have no relevance to the question.
- Amber: Events and policies that have some significance to the question.
- Green: Events and policies that are directly relevant to the question.

How extensive were the presidencies of Truman and Eisenhower in terms of social reform in the period 1945 to 1960?

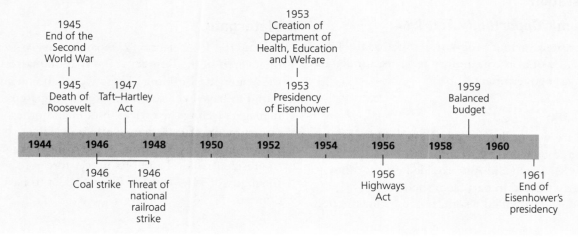

Domestic politics 1961–74: Kennedy, Johnson and Nixon REVISED

The 1960s saw considerable social reform, particularly with President Johnson's Great Society programme, although there was some retrenchment under the Republican president **Nixon**.

Kennedy and the New Frontier, 1961–63

John F. Kennedy was a Democrat with ambitious plans to improve people's lives through his New Frontier programme. This included **urban renewal**, medical care for the aged and a higher minimum wage. Unfortunately he was faced with a hostile Congress dominated by conservative Democrats and Republicans who vetoed most of his measures.

He was himself a fiscal conservative who was reluctant to increase government spending. As a result his administration seemed disappointing on the domestic front:

- Public works schemes costing $900 million were undertaken.
- He increased the minimum wage to $1.25 an hour.
- Measures were passed to help the long-term unemployed, such as the Manpower and Training Act to help them retrain.
- Social security benefits were extended.

Johnson and the Great Society

Kennedy's successor **Lyndon B. Johnson** was more ambitious on the domestic front. He declared war on poverty and introduced an extensive Great Society programme that was intended to transform the USA. It had two objectives:

- To give poorer people the wherewithal to improve their own lives.
- To provide them with direct help where necessary.

Legislation

Economic Opportunity Act, 1964

This created various programmes such as the Job Corps to work on community projects, funded by the federal government.

Medicare

Medicare was healthcare provision paid for out of taxes, and by federal government.

- The Medical Care Act provided care for the elderly funded in part from their taxes.
- Medicaid provided healthcare cover for the poor.

Elementary and Secondary Education Act, 1965

This marked the first time the federal authorities became involved in funding public education; the aim was to ensure provision was equal across the USA.

Failings of the Great Society

While the Great Society programme was comprehensive, its results were often disappointing:

- Money earmarked for its provision had to be diverted towards the cost of the Vietnam War (see page 86).
- States often diverted funds themselves away, for example, from education.
- Costs of provision were too high so coverage was often less than anticipated.

Nixon and Republican revival

President Nixon was far more interested in foreign affairs than domestic and was also a conservative who sought a reduced role of government. However, he did maintain many of the Great Society programmes but his biggest domestic issue was the economy, which suffered from increasing inflation. Nixon's response was the New Economic Policy:

- It aimed to reduce borrowing by forcing up interest rates.
- When this failed, in 1971 he introduced a 90-day prices and wages freeze and created a Pay Board and Price Commission to oversee these.

In fact inflation did slow and a 7.9 per cent devaluation of the dollar made US goods more competitive abroad.

After 1972, however, Nixon's government was dominated by the **Watergate** scandal to such an extent that it could hardly function in normal terms.

Watergate

During the 1972 election campaign, burglars were discovered in the **Democrat Party** headquarters in the Watergate Building. These were subsequently found to have been sent by Nixon's campaign managers to bug the offices. Nixon and other government officials denied all knowledge. However, the investigation of the scandal progressed to presidential level and Nixon was forced to resign in August 1974 – the only US president to have done so.

Quick quizzes at **www.hoddereducation.co.uk/myrevisionnotes**

How far do you agree?

Read the following extract and summarise each of its arguments. Use your knowledge to agree or contradict.

Arguments in extract	Knowledge that corroborates	Knowledge that contradicts
1		
2		
3		

EXTRACT

From John Morton Blum, Years of Discord: American Politics and Society 1961–1974, *published in 1991.*

The Council of Economic Advisors... began in 1967 to warn the president that total spending, domestic and military were creating deficits that would bring serious inflation unless taxes were raised... military spending in Vietnam created [this problem]. Domestic spending on anti-poverty measures was growing but remained insufficient. Redistributive taxation at a moderate rate could have reduced the shortfall. Both personal and political factors prevented that course. By 1967 Johnson lacked the votes in Congress for tax reform. He had never had any enthusiasm for it anyway. Indeed he lacked the votes even for a tax increase. And he had no intention of curtailing the war to contain military expenditures.

Without Lyndon Johnson, social reform in the 1960s might not have travelled as far as it did. But government under Johnson suffered from his personality. Obsessed about his place in history, he was in a rush, almost a frenzy, to build his record before the mandate of his victory in 1964 had run out. He believed he had no choice, and he was probably correct. But by hurrying legislation along he risked imprecision and ambiguity in the resulting statues... Johnson indulged in excesses of speech that promised more than anyone could deliver and boasted more than anyone could believe. No president could abolish poverty, but Johnson claimed he could and later that he almost had.

Developing an argument

Below are a sample essay question, a list of key points to be made in the essay, and a paragraph from the essay. Read the question, the plan and the sample paragraph. Rewrite the paragraph in order to develop an argument. Your paragraph should answer the question directly, and set out the evidence that supports your argument. Crucially, it should develop an argument by setting out a general answer to the question and reasons that support this.

'The Watergate scandal reversed the growing power of the presidency.' How far do you agree with this statement in respect to the role of the presidency in the period 1961 to 1974?

Key points

- Kennedy's social welfare programme was prevented from implementation by a hostile Congress.
- The impact of the Great Society programme was negated by the diverting of funds to pay for the Vietnam War.
- Nixon's second term was dominated by the Watergate scandal.
- Presidential power was reduced by a series of Acts after Watergate.

Sample paragraph

Presidential power had been growing since 1961. However, Kennedy could not get much of his ambitious social welfare legislation passed due to the hostility of Congress. Johnson was even more ambitious with his Great Society programme which he hoped would transform the USA. However, it suffered because the cost of the Vietnam War meant funds had to be diverted. Nixon sought a certain retrenchment in the role of the presidency and less legislation was proposed during his first term. However, his second term was dominated by the unfolding Watergate scandal and it was his misuse of power here that led to reductions in the powers of the presidency.

Economic change and developments

The post-war period saw a prosperity unprecedented in history in its range and longevity. However, while most Americans became better off as a result, it is important to remember it was not universal. Many African-Americans particularly in the South remained in poverty and there was considerable difference in wealth between states; again those of the South and the Appalachians remained relatively poor – in 1947, for example, 34 per cent of all Kentucky farms were worth less than $300.

The economic boom

By 1945, the USA, with 7 per cent of the world's population, enjoyed 42 per cent of its wealth. Per capita income at $1,450 was twice as high as that of Britain, one of its closest competitors. GNP had risen 35 per cent since 1945. Economic expansion led to greater employment opportunities for more of the population and a huge growth in consumerism.

The GI Bill of Rights

The GI Bill of Rights, also known as the Selective Servicemen's Readjustment Act, had been passed in 1944, offering grants to ex-servicemen for education or business enterprise. Eight million took up the offer. Its provisions were to be administered by the **Veterans' Association**. One provision was largely unnecessary: veterans were awarded $20 per week while looking for work: less than 20 per cent of the monies allocated for this were distributed because work was so plentiful to come by.

The provision of mortgages for veterans

The GI Bill of Rights also offered home loans to facilitate home ownership. They offered mortgages of up to 90 per cent of the cost, with interest rates as low as 4 per cent. Almost 2.4 million veterans took advantage of this, a significant factor in the development of widespread home ownership.

Home ownership

House construction expanded rapidly in the post-war years. 1n 1944, 114,000 family homes were built: by 1950 this figure had risen to 15 million.

The percentage of Americans owning their own homes rose from 50 to 60 per cent between 1950 and 1960. Many were in the suburbs, made possible by greater mobility.

This meant that many Americans gained space in their homes – space for gardens, garages and, above all, privacy. Home ownership came to symbolise the prosperity of ordinary Americans.

The growth of the suburbs

Many new homes were in suburbs on the outskirts of urban areas. The numbers living here grew from 17 per cent in 1920 to 33 per cent by 1960. Critics complained they lacked variety, but they did see new developments such as shopping malls – these grew from 8 in 1946 to over 4000 by the late 1950s.

The rise of consumer society

There was a rapid expansion in consumer spending fuelled by incessant advertising particularly on television – and by 1960 there were 50 million TV sets. Americans also spent considerable sums on white goods – by 1951, 90 per cent of US families had fridges and 75 per cent washing machines and telephones.

As before many of these goods were purchased on credit; the amount of debt increased from $5.7 billion in 1945 to $56.1 billion by 1960. Staying at home watching TV led to the development of frozen and convenience food while the desire for convenience generally led to items as diverse as Polaroid cameras and synthetic, easy-care fabrics.

One phenomenon was the baby boom, a rapid growth in numbers of children being born. Four million babies were born each year between 1954 and 1964. By 1957 nappies alone became a $500 million per year industry.

Extent of consumption

In the early 1950s the USA had 6 per cent of the world's population but consumed 33 per cent of all its goods. The average American had a lifestyle his/her parents could hardly have dreamed of.

Turning assertion into argument

Below are a series of definitions, a sample exam question and two sample conclusions. One of the conclusions achieves a high mark because it contains an argument. The other achieves a lower mark because it contains only description and assertion. Identify which is which. The mark scheme on page 7 will help you.

- **Description**: a detailed account.
- **Assertion**: a statement of fact or an opinion which is not supported by a reason.
- **Reason**: a statement which explains or justifies something.
- **Argument**: an assertion justified with a reason.

To what extent was there a genuine improvement in the living conditions of Americans during the period 1945 to 1960?

Student 1

There is clearly evidence that living standards improved during the period 1945 to 1960. The percentage of Americans owning their own homes, for example, rose from 50 to 60 per cent between 1950 and 1960. Many were in the suburbs, away from the pollution and overcrowding of the cities, made possible by greater mobility. The numbers living there grew from 17 per cent in 1920 to 33 per cent by 1960. Critics complained they lacked variety, but they did see new developments such as shopping malls — these grew from 8 in 1946 to over 4000 by the late 1950s. People spent more time at home. As a result there was a huge growth in consumer spending on the home. Television featured persuasive advertisements; by 1950 too there were 50 million TV sets. Viewers also spent considerable sums on white goods — by 1951, 90 per cent of US families had fridges and 75 per cent washing machines and telephones. Many of these goods were purchased on credit. In the early 1950s the USA had 6 per cent of the world's population but consumed 33 per cent of all its goods. The average American had a lifestyle his/her parents could hardly have dreamed of.

Student 2

There is clear evidence to show that living standards improved for many US groups during the period 1945 to 1960. This is particularly exemplified by house purchase which saw the numbers of home owners grow from 50 to 60 per cent between 1950 and 1960. However, the prosperity was not universal across the states or across ethnic groups –African-Americans particularly in the South remained poor while many in the Appalachian states still lacked basic amenities such as electricity. For those whose lives were improved, however, standards reached levels unimaginable during the pre-war years. The growth in private transport facilitated the movement into the suburbs where people stayed more in their homes, entertained by TV – 50 million sets by 1960 – and buying white consumer goods marketed extensively by TV advertising. However, many of these goods were bought on credit. Some feared that if the boom ended, consumers would be just as vulnerable to economic downturn as in the pre-war years.

Ideological, social, regional and ethnic divisions

For all the prosperity, significant divisions remained in US society. These were exacerbated in the 1950s by the communist witch-hunts, and the development of the Civil Rights movement.

McCarthyism

Joseph McCarthy was a Wisconsin Senator who in 1950 accused the **State Department** of being infested with 200 communist spies. Although he had no evidence to support his claims, this initiated a witch-hunt against public officials which culminated in an investigation of the armed forces. One of McCarthy's investigative techniques was the use of 'multiple untruth' by which his accusations were so complex it was difficult to refute them coherently. Mud sticks. McCarthy also had access to FBI files. He gained considerable support from:

- conservatives who were suspicious of new ideas
- church groups who associated communism with the work of the devil
- less well-educated and affluent members of society, many of whom were susceptible to conspiracy theories.

Loss of support

While McCarthy was successful at first in the widespread galvanising of public opinion, various factors lost him support:

- He lost credibility when his hearings were televised and viewers saw his drunken, bullying tactics.
- Many thought he had gone too far when he began to investigate the army for communist infiltration: it was embroiled at the time in the **Korean War**, fighting against communist forces.
- He became implicated in scandal in deferring military conscription for members of his own staff.

McCarthy was criticised by President Eisenhower for his attack on the army, censured by the Senate and drifted back into obscurity before dying of alcoholism in 1957 – but at its height, his committee had been popular, and such were the levels of fear that millions were prepared to believe his accusations.

Civil Rights

The Civil Rights movement gathered pace in the 1950s:

- In 1954 in Brown *v*. Board of Education of Topeka, the Supreme Court ruled that the notion of 'separate but equal' should not apply to schools. This set an important precedent for the desegregation of schools although it set no deadline and many areas in the South were slow to apply it – by 1957, 240,000 African-American children remained in segregated schools in the South.
- In 1957, in Arkansas, President Eisenhower had to send in the National Guard to protect African-American students as they attended the newly desegregated Little Rock High School.
- The Montgomery Bus Boycott 1955: African-Americans boycotted public transport to stop segregation of seating. In November 1956 the Supreme Court ruled that such segregation was unconstitutional.

Many protests and demonstrations were undertaken to highlight the extent of discrimination and the level of violence which white opponents of Civil Rights were prepared to use.

Freedom Rides and Freedom Marches

In the early 1960s the Congress of Racial Equality (CORE) organised 'freedom rides' in which volunteers tested the resolve of segregation in the South by sitting in white-only areas on public transport and at rest stops. They were met by arrest and even murder – but in September the Interstate Commerce Commission (see page 30) insisted bus terminals everywhere be desegregated.

- Elsewhere there were mass marches and protests about segregation. Many of them were led by Dr **Martin Luther King Jr**, the leading figure in the Civil Rights movement, and organised by the Student Non-Violent Coordinating Committee (SNCC).
- In 1965 King decided to march from Selma, Alabama, to present a petition demanding voting rights be upheld. It was met with considerable brutality.

Civil Rights activities resulted in the following legislation:

- Civil Rights Act 1964, banning discrimination in public places.
- Voting Rights Act 1965, to ensure voting procedures were carried out fairly and no one entitled to vote could be refused.

However, laws weren't always obeyed. Many African-Americans grew impatient with non-violent protest and joined more militant groups which advocated '**Black Power**'. This was particularly the case after the assassination of Dr King in April 1968, which resulted in widespread unrest across US cities.

RAG – rate the interpretation

Read the following interpretation and, using three coloured pens, shade the text to show the following:

- Red: Shade anything you disagree with in red.
- Amber: Shade anything you partly agree/disagree with in amber.
- Green: Shade the sections you agree with in green.

EXTRACT A

From Paul Levine and Harry Papasotiriou, America Since 1945: The American Moment, *published in 2005.*

Senator Joseph McCarthy entered the red-baiting game in February 1950 when he began making claims about a list of 205, or 57, or 81 communists in the State Department (the number kept changing). His claims were unsubstantiated or at best relied on information revealed years earlier. Yet they captured the public mood so well as to turn him into one of the most prominent politicians in America. His unsubstantiated allegations therefore became very potent politically, raising new fears in the public about disloyalty after three years of Truman's loyalty programme and five years of the FBI's spy hunts. The Truman administration had no choice to strike back at him, even though it thereby helped to raise him to national prominence. Once the battle was joined between McCarthy and the Truman administration, it divided Congress mainly among partisan lines [by political party] with the Republican leadership in effect using him to strike at the five-term Democratic rule...

McCarthy rarely focused much on actual communist threats, such as the Soviet Union and China, and he never uncovered even a single spy. Instead he railed against imaginary, hidden enemies...

Develop the detail   a

Below are a sample exam question and a paragraph written in answer to this question. The paragraph contains a limited amount of detail. Annotate the paragraph to add additional detail to the answer.

To what extent did the Civil Rights movement improve the lives of African-Americans between 1955 and 1970?

The Civil Rights movement improved the lives of African-Americans to a certain extent. It fought against segregation. It had some notable successes in the 1950s, for example the Montgomery Bus Boycott. However, there was considerable resentment against school desegregation and sometimes US troops had to be sent to ensure this was achieved. In the early 1960s many went on 'freedom rides' to try to end segregation on public transport and rest rooms. Others marched to win political rights, for example in Selma in 1965. They were often met by brutality and violence. Even when Civil Rights were achieved, inequalities remained and it was these which led to severe rioting between 1964 and 1966.

Youth culture, and protest and the mass media

The 1950s and 1960s saw the development of significant youth culture. The 1960s moreover saw significant youth protest. People spoke of a 'generation gap', or conflict between young and older people, but there were also tensions between different groups of young people themselves.

Youth culture

Most of the post-war population was young: in 1950, 41.6 per cent of the population was under 24. Many teenagers had jobs and surplus income with a market to cater for their interests. They had discrete fashions, music, films.

Reactions from older people

Many older people feared the breakdown of deference and authority, seeing young people as violent and anti-social.

Rock and roll

Fears were exacerbated by the beginnings of rock and roll music which was decried in part because it originated from black rhythm and blues and was very different from the crooning and sentimental ballads of the war years.

However, the initial cohort of rock and roll artists such as Elvis Presley tended to reinvent themselves as mainstream entertainers as the popularity of the genre declined. By the early 1960s youth culture seemed largely non-threatening. Young people seemed content to enjoy their prosperity.

Youth culture in the 1960s

Youth culture changed as the 1960s progressed, from more specific fashions aimed at young people to the massive expansion of the popular music industry. Here trends became much more different to those listened to by their parents – such as 'beat music' imported from the UK and later on psychedelic music often influenced by drugs. However, young people also began to protest, to reject their parents' society.

Protest and the mass media

Many young people opposed a society which they saw as conservative and materialistic. Some formed groups which actively sought alternative lifestyles, such as 'hippies', while there was widespread opposition to the war in Vietnam (see page 86). Some young people advocated violent revolution as exemplified by the 'Weathermen' group who committed terrorist atrocities.

Hippies

Hippies sought alternative lifestyles, often living in 'communes'. They were recognisable by long hair, flowing clothes and often a liberal attitude to illicit drugs. They tended to resent authority and often came into conflict with the police.

Student protest

Youth protest was particularly associated with students and universities. The Students for a Democratic Society (SDS) wrote the Port Huron Manifesto in 1962, calling for a fairer society. They went on to organise 'sit-ins' and protests often on their university campuses. Students supported issues such as Civil Rights and greater economic equality and opposed in particular military expansion and the war in Vietnam. In 1969, 700,000 students marched on Washington to protest against the war.

Impact of youth protest

Youth protest shocked many older people who could not understand their rejection of their comfortable lifestyles – although more came to share their criticism of involvement in Vietnam. Their main impact was in mass media coverage – their protests received wide coverage. People saw young people protesting about something on the televisions most evenings and read about them in their newspapers. In particular the media became fascinated by hippies and their lifestyles. It was interesting – and guaranteed to anger and threaten many of the older generation. It may be that for example, the Vietnam protests did influence government thinking.

Kent State

In 1970 the National Guard fired on protestors at Kent State University in Ohio, killing four students. This shocked many people, and 2 million students went on strike in protest.

Divisions in youth opinion

For most teenagers, rebellion against authority was a phase they went through. Even at the time there were tensions between those who supported the US lifestyle and indeed the war in Vietnam and saw hippies and others as unpatriotic and traitors, and those who chose to protest. Most young people obeyed the draft to fight in Vietnam and resented those who did not.

! Summarise the arguments a

Below are a sample essay question and one of the extracts referred to in the question. You must read the extract and identify the interpretation offered. Look for the arguments of the passage.

With reference to the extract and your contextual knowledge, how convincing do you find the extract in relation to the extent of youth protest in the 1960s?

Interpretation offered by the extract:

_____

_____

EXTRACT

From Thomas C. Reeves, Twentieth Century America: A Brief History, _published in 2000._

America had known 'rebellious youth' in the 1920s and beatniks in the 1950s. But in the Johnson–Nixon years, a storm of dissent coming largely from upper-middle-class young people shook the country as never before. Critics blamed this left-wing rebellion on prosperity, mounting secularism, parental permissiveness, and a breakdown in schools. Others saw it as a praiseworthy crusade, striking out against repressive and irrational laws and institutions and heralding the dawn of a glorious new era of peace and love. The movement preceded serious American involvement in the Vietnam War but that conflict fuelled the rebellion and propelled it into a force that significantly altered American culture.

The seeds of rebellion could be seen in 1962 when 59 delegates of the leftist Students for a Democratic Society issued the Port Huron Statement. This 60-page manifesto, written by activist Tom Hayden and others, seriously criticised American governmental and economic institutions and called for more freedom and democracy, and declared that 'America should concentrate on its genuine social priorities: abolish squalor, terminate neglect and establish an environment for people to live with dignity and creativeness'.

⚡ Spectrum of importance

Below are a sample essay question and a list of general points which could be used to answer the question. Use your own knowledge and the information on the opposite page to reach a judgement about the importance of these general points to the question posed. Write numbers on the spectrum below to indicate their relative importance. Having done this, write a brief justification of your placement, explaining why some of these factors are more important than others. The resulting diagram could form the basis of an essay plan.

'Genuine criticisms of inequalities in American society were at the heart of youth revolt in the 1960s.' How far do you agree with this statement?

1 Youth culture and the 'generation gap'

2 Phase of development into adulthood

3 SDS and the Port Huron Manifesto

4 Involvement in Civil Rights

5 Hippies

6 Protest about the Vietnam War

⟵———————————————————————————————⟶
Least important   Most important

The USA and international relations

The foreign policies of the USA in the post-war years were dominated by the development of the **Cold War** and relations with the USSR.

The Cold War

After the Second World War, the USA became worried by the increasing influence and expansion of the USSR, who first forced countries in Eastern Europe to become communist and then sought to extend their influence in the wider world. This became more dangerous after 1949 when both nations had nuclear weapons. In the period 1945 to 1963, there were various crises which could have escalated into direct conflict between the two superpowers.

The Berlin Airlift, 1948–49

Post-war Germany and its capital Berlin had been divided between the Allies. When the Russians tried to take over the whole of Berlin by means of a blockade in 1948, an airlift was organised to fly in supplies.

NATO

The North Atlantic Treaty Organisation (NATO) was formed after the Berlin crisis of 1948–49. This was an alliance of western European nations, including the USA, against Soviet aggression.

The Korean War, 1950–53

Korea had been divided between the communist North and capitalist South. When North Korea invaded the South, the UN sent a force, dominated by the US military, to defeat their action. The war escalated with the involvement of communist China, but peace was agreed before the USSR became directly involved.

The Cuban Missile Crisis, 1962

In 1962, the USSR built nuclear sites on Cuba, its client state only 90 miles off the coast of the USA. President Kennedy imposed a blockade. It seemed nuclear confrontation was likely: only at the last minute was a settlement reached.

Relations with USSR and China

Relations with the USSR and China were at the heart of the Cold War. After the Russian leader, Stalin, died in 1953, relations with the USSR seemed to improve with the thaw. However, it was the change in relations with China which really seemed to reduce the intensity of the Cold War.

The thaw

Both sides feared the destructive power of their nuclear arsenals and realised no one could really win a nuclear war. The new USSR leader, Khrushchev, seemed more reasonable, and met both Presidents Eisenhower and Kennedy in a series of summits. Commentators spoke of a thaw in hostility – however, there remained significant disagreements:

- The **Space Race** developed and the nuclear arsenals continued to grow.
- Berlin became a flash-point with the construction of the **Berlin Wall** in 1961.
- The Cuban Missile Crisis threatened all-out nuclear war.

After Cuba, attempts were made to reduce the amounts of nuclear weapons with the Partial Test Ban Treaty of 1963 but tensions remained.

Relations with China

China had become communist in 1949, and had fought against UN troops in Korea. However, it had poor relations with the USSR. In the late 1960s President Nixon realised he could exploit this to reduce Cold War tensions.

In 1971, the USA improved its relations with China, initially by lifting a trade embargo. This was followed by direct talks and a visit to Peking by President Nixon. As relations improved with China, the USSR feared an alliance against them – so the USSR too sought to improve relations. The result was *détente*.

Détente, 1969–75

The period of *détente* saw two key agreements:

- Strategic Arms Limitations Treaty (SALT) 1971 – this was the first formal agreement to limit the number of nuclear weapons held by the USA and USSR.
- Helsinki Agreements 1975 – these agreements guaranteed basic civil rights and eliminated potential flash-points in Europe emanating from the Second World War – notably agreements between West and East Germany.

Below are a sample exam question and a timeline. Read the question, study the timeline and, using three coloured pens, put a Red, Amber or Green star next to the events to show:

● Red: Events and policies that have no relevance to the question.
● Amber: Events and policies that have some significance to the question.
● Green: Events and policies that are directly relevant to the question.

To what extent were the USA and USSR engaged in Cold War during the period 1945 to 1975?

i **Concluding an argument**

Look at the key points of the answer below.

1 How effective is the proposed conclusion?

2 Could it be improved – especially in relation to Level 5 answers?

'The relations between the USA and USSR in the period 1945 to 1975 were dominated by hostility.' Assess the validity of this statement.

Key points
● Development of the Cold War
● The thaw
● Fear of nuclear war
● Cuban Missile Crisis
● Development of *détente*

Conclusion

Hostility dominated relations between the USA and USSR. It had led to Cold War and seen crises such as the Berlin Airlift, Korean War and Cuban Missile Crisis. Nevertheless from the 1950s there was a growing realisation that if hostility developed into actual conflict, no one could win and therefore tensions eased through the policy of détente, which saw the SALT 1 treaty to reduce nuclear weapons and Helsinki Agreements to reduce tensions in Europe. The picture then is not one of complete hostility – relations improved with détente.

The Vietnam War

One reason why the USA was so anxious to reduce Cold War tensions in the 1960s and 1970s was because of its preoccupation with the Vietnam War.

Background to US involvement

Vietnam is a country in south-east Asia. Like Korea, it had been divided into a communist North and capitalist South. The government in the South was very unpopular with the mainly peasant population in the North who supported a communist guerrilla movement in the South called the Vietcong.

From the late 1950s, the US unsuccessfully sent advisors to help the South Korean forces. In 1963 they became involved in a coup against the unpopular leader Van Diem. This was followed by a succession of military dictators, none of whom appeared either effective in fighting the Vietcong or popular with the South Vietnamese people. Despite US efforts, the Vietcong appeared to be gaining ever more ground. Overall the USA was becoming more and more involved in the conflict.

Full-scale US involvement

President Johnson was told that South Vietnam would not survive without wholesale US military involvement. In August 1964 he used a naval attack on a US destroyer in the Gulf of Tonkin to persuade Congress to agree to full-scale deployment of US troops. In 1965 he agreed to the large-scale bombing of North Vietnam with Operation Rolling Thunder.

Responses to involvement in Vietnam

Despite US involvement, the communist forces, now including regular North Vietnamese forces, continued to gain. The USA became divided as to support or oppose the war. Many young people opposed it – but others enlisted readily. However, more people became disillusioned as the war dragged on and the numbers of US deaths mounted – reaching 50,000 in total.

Reasons for US lack of success

- It was difficult for regular troops to fight guerrillas who were concealed in local villages and fought largely from ambush.
- US troops became bitter and frustrated – sometimes responding brutally, as with the My Lai massacre of March 1968 when 347 people in a village which allegedly supported the Vietcong were killed by US troops.
- The 1968 Tet Offensive helped destroy US resolve. Here the communist forces launched a surprise offensive which saw them temporarily gain control of 75 per cent of South Vietnam. Although the offensive eventually failed, its impact on US morale was devastating.
- Many veterans returned home traumatised and ready to talk of the horrors of the war.

The role of the mass media

Vietnam was the first full-scale war to be televised. Hence Americans could see the realities of the conflict on the news in their homes each evening. Although up to the time of the Tet Offensive, the media was broadly supportive of the war, people could see the US was not winning. The widespread introduction of colour TV moreover brought home the horrors of war.

After Tet the US media became more critical. Television showed US troops fighting the Vietcong in the grounds of the US Embassy – supposedly the most secure place in Vietnam. In 1972 the effects of **napalm bombing** were shown as a nine-year-old girl fled with her back on fire. All these examples showed the power of the media to influence opinion, and it helped turn more and more Americans against the war.

Nixon

President Nixon was committed to withdrawing the USA from Vietnam, but he still hoped for a South Vietnamese victory.

- He introduced the idea of **Vietnamisation** whereby South Vietnam would take on more responsibility for fighting with US support.
- Peace talks began in Paris.

Escalation by the invasion of Cambodia

In May 1970, Nixon also escalated tension by the invasion of neighbouring Cambodia and Laos, which the North were using for supply routes. This only served to trigger a communist revolt in Cambodia led by the **Khmer Rouge**.

US troops became more and more disenchanted, particularly as they knew the war was coming to an end and were unwilling to risk their lives unnecessarily.

US withdrawal

US forces withdrew from Vietnam in 1972; three years later the North completed its conquest of the South. The Vietnam War was widely seen as a disaster for the USA.

! Eliminate irrelevance · a

Below are a sample exam question and a paragraph written in answer to this question. Read the paragraph and identify the parts that are not directly relevant to the question. Draw a line through the information that is irrelevant and justify your deletions in the margin.

> To what extent did involvement in the Vietnamese War cause political tensions in the USA in the years 1954 to 1972?

Interestingly this was ordered by Kennedy, who was himself to be assassinated soon afterwards. The Vietnamese War was to cause significant political tensions as US involvement escalated and little progress appeared to be made, but this was very much a phenomenon of the period 1965 onwards rather than the whole period covered by the question. The US began to send advisors, for example from the mid-1950s onwards, but the war attracted comparatively little attention in the media until the escalation following the Gulf of Tonkin incident of 1964. Here North Vietnamese torpedo boats were alleged to have fired on a US destroyer. Even when the USA had become involved in a coup against the unpopular South Vietnamese leader Diem in November 1963 most Americans were unaware of Vietnam.

ⵜ RAG – rate the factors · a

Below are a sample essay question and a list of factors. Read the question, study the timeline and, using three coloured pens, put a Red, Amber or Green star next to the events to show:

- Red: Events and policies that have no relevance to the question.
- Amber: Events and policies that have some significance to the question.
- Green: Events and policies that are directly relevant to the question.

> 'The main reason for the withdrawal of US forces in Vietnam was the hostile media coverage of the war.' How far do you agree with this statement?

Factors

US support for South Vietnam in the 1950s/early 1960s

Coup against Diem 1963

Escalation of US involvement 1965

Tet Offensive 1968

End of Johnson's presidency 1968

Television coverage

Nixon becoming president 1969

Policy of Vietnamisation 1969

Popular protest

Paris Peace talks

Invasion of Cambodia 1970

Kent State shootings 1970

Watergate scandal 1972–74

North Vietnamese victory 1975

The USA by 1975

The USA remained by far the most powerful nation in the world but it was still rent by social divisions.

The place of the USA as a superpower

The USA was a superpower with huge influence in the world, as exemplified by its continued involvement in struggles against communist expansion, for example in Africa. However, it eschewed direct action; for example, Congress refused to allow military aid in Angola in 1974 or help for South Vietnam in the final stages of the conflict.

Continued US influence

The USA continued to exert its influence, however. It maintained its NATO commitments with thousands of troops stationed in Europe, it became involved to try to bring about peace in the Middle East and continued to build nuclear weapons. *Détente* continued, including closer co-operation with the USSR such as the 1975 Apollo-Soyuz link-up in space.

The economy

The US economy had been hurt by the 1973 **oil crisis**. In 1973 oil cost $2–3 a barrel; by 1976 this had risen to $12. As in other developed countries this marked the end of post-war prosperity. By 1974, the USA was hit by recession; unemployment grew and inflation reached 9 per cent. President Ford agreed tax cuts to try to stimulate spending but opposed kick-starting economic growth by public works schemes. This in a sense marked the end of the public spending solutions to economic problems that had been in place since the New Deal.

The government indeed favoured voluntary schemes to improve the economy such as the Whip Inflation Now campaign which saw little tangible action.

The impact of Watergate

Ford angered many people by his pardon of former president Nixon in September 1974. He may have felt it important to close the Watergate scandal and move on, but many Americans thought Nixon should have been brought to account.

The limits of social cohesion

The USA remained socially divided.

Amnesty

President Ford offered pardons to draft dodgers and deserters if they would agree to two years' public service, for example in community programmes. Although this was, like the presidential pardon above, designed to bind wounds, many resented it – included those whose loved ones had served and died or returned home maimed.

Social cohesion

Issues such as Vietnam continued to divide Americans. There were still divisions between the generations, within generations themselves and different ethnic groups. The West and South still felt grievances against the North – the South in particular was coming to terms with dramatic changes in race relations. By 1975 many Americans felt less confident as a result of the reverses of the 1960s and 1970s.

However, many Americans continued to enjoy prosperity: 48 per cent of households owned at least one car and almost 80 per cent owned a TV. TV in particular helped standardise views across the nation. People generally were more tolerant, less racist and sexist – although there were still inequalities and real concerns.

Other social changes

- An increasing divorce rate:
  - The 1970s saw the divorce rate increase 66 per cent; from 1975 a million marriages ended in divorce each year.
  - Most divorces were initiated by discontented wives.
- A rise in religious belief, specifically Christian:
  - While the family seemed in decline, religious belief for many increased. This was aided by the development of **television evangelism** – charismatic religious leaders such as Billy Graham and Jerry Falwell saw their audience grow in millions.
  - The surge in religion became allied to a growth in conservative politics both at federal, state and local level. For example, some local education authorities banned books which were felt to be anti-Christian or insisted creationism be taught alongside evolution.
  - The 'Moral Majority' was to become a significant force in politics by the late 1970s.
- A growing awareness of environmentalism. The 1960s and 1970s saw more concern for the environment; in 1970, 20 million Americans participated in 'Earth Day'. Legislation included:
  - the 1969 National Environmental Policy Act which committed government to improving the environment
  - the setting up in 1970 of the Environment Protection Agency to achieve this: by 1973 its budget exceeded $2.5 billion.

! Mind map

Read the question and complete the mind map to identify relevant reasons. Then prioritise your reasons by adding numbers to each box – with 1 as the most important reason and 6 as the least important.

'The impact of Watergate was the main cause of political tensions in the USA by 1975.' Assess the validity of this statement.

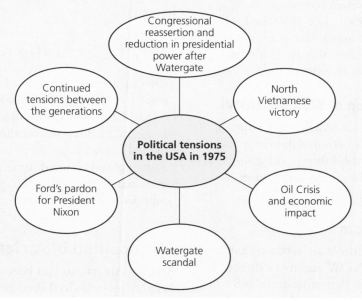

! Developing an argument

Below are a sample essay title, a list of key points to be made in the essay, and a paragraph from the essay. Read the question, the plan and the sample paragraph. Rewrite the paragraph in order to develop an argument. Your paragraph should answer the question directly, and set out the evidence that supports your argument. Crucially, it should develop an argument by setting out a general answer to the question and reasons that support this.

How accurate is it to say that political tensions threatened the power of the presidency by 1975?

Key points

- Reduction in presidential powers after Watergate
- Continued political global influence of USA
- Congress refused funding to forestall a North Vietnamese victory
- Tensions caused by pardon for Nixon
- Continued tensions between generations.

Sample paragraph

Political tensions continued to divide the USA and threaten the power of the presidency to a certain extent. After Watergate, various constraints had been placed on presidential power, for example the War Powers Act, which was deployed to prevent President Ford sending aid to South Vietnam to try to forestall North Vietnamese victory in 1975. The USA was considerably divided over Ford's pardon for Nixon. Many felt Nixon should be punished like his aides, many of whom were imprisoned. Other tensions continued, such as the 'generation gap' where young people questioned the decisions of their elders. However, while this was clearly a political tension, it did not threaten the power of the presidency so it would negate the statement.

New cultural developments

The USA changed culturally, often in conflicting ways.

The role of women

The role and status of women had changed dramatically since the 1950s. The 1960s had seen a more aggressive feminist movement as exemplified by the activities of the National Association of Women and **second wave feminism**.

National Organisation of Women (NOW)

Consisting mainly of white middle-class women, this was formed in 1966 to combat discrimination; by the early 1970s its membership stood at 40,000 and it had been involved in many court cases concerning women's rights.

Second wave feminism

This movement, often known as 'Women's Lib', was less organised than NOW and more direct. Supporters participated in demonstrations and actions to promote women's issues. However, the movement was too broad to be really successful. It embraced a range of views, from those of women who simply wanted a fairer deal in the workplace to extreme feminists such as the Society for Cutting Up Men (SCUM) in 1967. As a whole, therefore, second wave feminism lacked cohesion.

Women did, however, make considerable gains such as equal rights guaranteed by the Supreme Court in 1973, and abortion, legalised in the Roe *v.* Wade case in the same year. More women joined the professions and expected to be equal partners in marriage and 86 per cent of college-educated women were in the workforce while between 1970 and 1974 the numbers of women in medical, law and business schools doubled.

Nevertheless there was still some way to go. Many men (and women) rejected feminism ideas and discrimination continued; for example, most states refused to ratify the 1973 Equal Rights Amendment, and, despite equal pay having legal enforcement in 1963, women still on average earned only 73 per cent of men's wages in 1975 while doing the same job.

Phyllis Schlafly and STOP ERA

One influential defender of traditional gender roles was Phyllis Schlafly whose organisation STOP ERA focused on opposition to the Equal Rights Amendment and abortion. Her movement gained considerable support from conservative elements and claimed some responsibility for the eventual failure of ERA to gain sufficient state support to become a constitutional amendment.

The position of African-Americans

African-Americans had become more assertive by 1975. Although Civil Rights legislation had been passed (see page 80), for many it was not enough or not sufficiently enforced. The 1960s had seen the development of movements such as Black Power, the more extreme of which advocated separation from whites. The Black Panthers, a paramilitary organisation, briefly took over the policing of many African-American communities.

Despite the law, many African-Americans still faced discrimination in 1975; teenage unemployment was often as high as 50 per cent while a similar percentage failed to graduate from school. Their average income still remained considerably less than that of their white counterparts. Nevertheless, there was a growing African-American middle class, and far more were employed in the professions. The 1970s saw the growth of African-American mayors and senior public officials. However, in 1980 there were only 18 African-Americans in Congress.

RAG – rate the interpretation

Read the following interpretation and, using three coloured pens, shade the text to show the following:

- Red: Shade anything you disagree with in red.
- Amber: Shade anything you partly agree/disagree with in amber.
- Green: Shade the sections you agree with in green.

EXTRACT

From David Reynolds, America, Empire of Liberty: A New History, *published in 2009.*

... although many feminists regarded Schlafly with near hatred as a cynical opportunist .. she tapped deep into American society. Her campaign against the ERA did not deny continued discrimination against women, especially in employment, but argued that this could be addressed through existing legislation. Passing ERA, Schlafly claimed, would deprive women of their freedom to be women and the laws that guaranteed this. Instead the ERA would impose 'a doctrinaire equality under which women must be treated the same as men'. Schlafly asserted it would 'take away from girls their exemption to the draft and their legal protection against predatory males. It will take away from wives and mothers their right to be provided with a home and financial support from their husbands. It will take away from senior women their extra social security benefits. It will take away a woman's present freedom of choice to take a job – or to be a full-time wife and mother. In short, it will take away the right to be a woman.'

ERA supporters strenuously contested Schlafly's interpretation of what the amendment would do to women's rights, but they were slow to organise their campaign. Schlafly's STOP ERA ... did indeed halt the momentum to ratification in the mid-1970s.

Recommended reading

- John Morton Blum, *Years of Discord: American Politics and Society 1961–74* (1992)
- Eric F. Goldman, *The Crucial Decade – and After 1945–1960* (1960)
- Paul Levine and Harry Papasotiriou, *America Since 1945: The American Movement* (2005), Parts 1, 2, 3 and 4
- Thomas C. Reeves, *Twentieth Century America: A Brief History* (2000), Chapters 1–11

Exam focus (A-level)

Below are three extracts and a sample essay. Read it and the comments around it.

Using your understanding of the historical context, assess how convincing the arguments in these three extracts are in relation to US involvement in the conflict in Vietnam in the 1950s and 1960s.

EXTRACT A

From Thomas C. Reeves, Twentieth Century America: A Brief History, *published in 2000.*

By 1954, the United States was paying nearly 80 per cent of the cost of France's war in Vietnam. The administration considered sending troops and using atomic weapons to preserve French authority. But these moves lacked support from Congress and the nation's allies and the president chose not to intervene directly. On 7 May 1954, the French were defeated after a prolonged battle at the city of Dien Bien Phu.

A peace conference in Geneva that summer, in which the United States did not officially participate, produced the Geneva Accords. Vietnam was to be divided temporarily at the seventeenth parallel, Ho Chi Minh ruling the north and a pro-Western government in the south. Elections held in 1956 were to determine the country's future. The Eisenhower administration, fearful of a communist victory, responded by creating the South-East Asia Treaty Organisation. SEATO was an anti-communist alliance...

By the end of the Eisenhower years ... South Vietnam was in civil war. Between 1955 and 1961 the United States poured more than a billion dollars into South Vietnam, most of it in military aid. American leaders were determined to prevent the falling dominoes [countries falling to communism]. Senator John F. Kennedy used different metaphors in 1956 with the same meaning: 'Vietnam represents the cornerstone of the free world in south-east Asia, the keystone to the arch, the finger in the dyke.'

EXTRACT B

From Paul Levine and Harry Papasotiriou, America Since 1945: The American Moment, *published in 2005.*

The situation in South Vietnam was going from bad to worse after the overthrow of Diem in November 1963. A series of coups and other violent domestic confrontations, apart from the struggle against the Vietcong, rocked South Vietnam until 1967, when at least a stable government emerged under General Nguyen Van Thieu. The communist insurgency was gathering strength, challenging the government's authority in many provinces to the point where villages often paid taxes to the Vietcong. Without an American military presence, South Vietnam would probably have collapsed in 1965.

Johnson was aware that he was trapped, yet he dare not withdraw. Feeling out of his depth in foreign policy, he was reluctant to clash with the internationalist consensus that had supported a worldwide anti-communist crusade since 1950. He kept the entire Kennedy foreign policy team and was unwilling to countermand their policies that had led to a deeper American commitment to Vietnam in the first place.

EXTRACT C

From Niall Ferguson, Colossus, *published in 2004.*

Lack of clarity about America's aims in Vietnam, lack of confidence that these could be achieved quickly and lack of conviction that the stated aims were worth prolonged sacrifice: these were what caused public support for the war to slide as the body count rose inexorably towards its cumulative total, which was not far short of 50,000.

It is hard to say what was cause and which effect. Was it the declining popularity of the war that persuaded Lyndon Johnson to seek a negotiated peace, or was it the other way around? There are those who would argue that American society by the 1960s was simply incapable of pursuing such a war to a successful conclusion. But there is a strong case to be made for a lack of effective political leadership. Johnson simply failed to make the case for war either to the public or to Congress. Worse, as early as Christmas 1965 he embarked on a strategy of seeking peace negotiations by suspension of the air war against Hanoi. This gambit, repeated in September 1967, proved disastrous. By indicating American readiness to accept a compromise peace it encouraged North Vietnam to keep fighting while creating an expectation in the United States that an end to the war was in sight. It is no coincidence that public disapproval of the war overtook public approval the following month.

Extract A offers background information on the US involvement in Vietnam, showing that it was already significantly involved before the French withdrew, paying in fact 80 per cent of their costs. However, it argues that President Eisenhower chose not to intervene directly – possibly a reflection on the war in Korea which had been fought over similar issues and ending just a year earlier. Eisenhower's foreign policy priorities may have been USSR expansion in Europe but there was no appetite for further full-scale involvement in Asia. Nevertheless Eisenhower sought to prevent further communist encroachment in Asia with the creation of SEATO, a defensive alliance. The extract goes on to show that the United States, its reluctance notwithstanding, nevertheless was getting more and more embroiled in the conflict in Vietnam – a billion dollars, mainly in military aid. The point is emphasised by the reference to Kennedy who would subsequently as president continue Eisenhower's policy of aid to South Vietnam. Kennedy argues effectively that Vietnam is the front line in the war against communist expansion in Asia. This extract argues convincingly why the USA was becoming dragged into the conflict and is strong in showing it was a comparatively long-standing process – indeed almost at the same time as the full-scale war in Korea. It also shows the difference in technologies – Eisenhower could contemplate using nuclear weapons against the army of a developing country.

Wider context.

Understands author's reason for use for Kennedy as an example.

Explains why extract is convincing.

The extract does not, however, offer the impact, if any, of the US advisors and military aid. It explains why they became involved but not how or how effectively, or indeed how the people of the United States reacted.

Strikes balance.

Extract B argues that, despite US involvement, South Vietnam was being lost to the communists. It shows the ineffectiveness of US policy before full-scale involvement. The USA had been involved in the coup against Diem, but it was a further four years before a stable government emerged – and then under a military dictator, Thieu. It also shows that the Vietcong effectively ruled great swathes of the countryside, controlling villages which paid taxes to them rather than the government in Saigon. This explains in part why the US found it so difficult to fight the war on the ground. The Vietcong used the villages they controlled for support and shelter, and could blend into the landscape so US troops had no idea who their enemy actually was. This was to lead to frustrations resulting in tragic events such as the My Lai massacre.

Context is rather distant from the extract. Extract could be more closely followed.

The extract also explains Johnson's invidious position. He was an expert on domestic policy with ambitious schemes for a 'Great Society'. He had relatively little understanding of foreign policy but realised early on in his presidency that Vietnam would loom large. The extract shows that he could not withdraw. He continued Kennedy's policy and kept his predecessor's advisors. Although the policy of increasing involvement had not worked, it would nevertheless continue. This extract might have convinced more had it gone on to explain how Johnson actually escalated involvement after the Gulf of Tonkin incident in August 1964 – because Johnson, the president who would have preferred, if it was at all possible, to withdraw from Vietnam, was also the one who instigated full-scale US involvement.

Provides valid context.

Gives balance.

Extract C explains why public support for the war diminished. It argues that the original war aims lacked clarity and cohesion – indeed developing the argument in Extract B about Johnson's position. It mentions the rising body count, a factor which undoubtedly lost public support as more troops were killed for apparently little success. However, the second paragraph really argues convincingly of Johnson's dilemma. Not only did he fail to make a convincing case for war – perhaps unsurprisingly as he was unsure about the aims himself beyond the prevention of communism in south-east Asia and the maintenance of US prestige – but his policies were contradictory and played into the hands of the North Vietnamese. If he had put out peace feelers as early as Christmas 1965, this sent a message that the USA was tiring of war – both to the enemy and the public at home. This had the effect of galvanising the enemy into more ambitious military activity and conversely persuaded Americans that an end to the conflict was in sight – and implicitly that there was little point in continuing the fight. It was this dichotomy which caused public disapproval to grow.

Confident explanation of why extract convinces.

This is a very good response which gets to the heart of the extracts and explains not only why they convince but how they could have been even more convincing. However, the context on Extract B grows rather distant and not entirely related to the extract. This may have led to minor limitations in depth and breadth of Extract B, which means this answer would gain a high Level 4.

Moving from a Level 4 to Level 5

The exam focus essay on pages 50–51 provided a Level 5 essay. The response here achieves a Level 4. Read both responses, and the examiner's comments provided. Then work out how the answer on Vietnam could become Level 5.

Glossary

Alphabet agencies Term given to the agencies set up during the New Deal to address issues, so-called because they were known by their initials.

Anarchism A political creed which does not believe in organised government.

Anti-semitism Dislike of Jewish people.

Berlin Wall A wall that divided East and West Berlin, built by the communist East German government in August 1961.

Black Codes Codes of practice discriminating against black Americans.

Black Power Movement dating from the mid-1960s to give more power and rights to African-American people through their own efforts.

Bull market Stock market in which there is lots of confidence and lots of buying and selling.

Carpetbaggers The name given to emigrants from the North during Reconstruction whose motives were sometimes altruistic and at other times born out of greed.

Cold War Hostility without direct fighting; term used to describe relations between the USA and its allies, and the USSR and its allies between 1945 and 1989.

Communes Where people lived co-operatively together in small communities.

Communism A political philosophy that endorses a state-controlled economy and rewards people according to their perceived value to economy and society.

Compromise of 1877 The agreement by which Southern politicians would support Hays for president following the contested 1876 election – in return for the ending of Reconstruction.

Confederate Term given to the South after it broke away from the United States.

Congress The legislative body of the USA, comprising the House of Representatives representing all the citizens, and the Senate, representing the states. It can both initiate legislation and discuss any initiated by the president.

Deflation Where prices fall and the value of money therefore rises.

Democrat Political party supporting greater government intervention and traditionally appealing to a wider cross-section of society than the Republicans.

Détente Term to describe the reduction in Cold War tensions from 1969 to 1975 as exemplified by the 1972 SALT 1 treaty.

Fireside chats Roosevelt's radio addresses to the electorate.

Fiscal conservative Someone supporting the position of lower public spending, lower taxes and lower government debt.

Flappers Term given to fun-loving young women in the 1920s.

'Furlough babies' Babies conceived during wartime while their fathers were on leave from the armed forces.

Ghettos Poor areas of cities where people of a particular ethnic group were concentrated.

Gold standard A system by which the value of money is based on the amount of gold in the nation's reserves.

Good Neighbour US foreign policy of being friendly with countries of Latin and South America.

Granger movement Movement of farmers co-operating to purchase farm machinery and the sale of their products, to cut out middle men.

Gross domestic product (GDP) The total value of goods produced and services provided in a country.

Great Migration Term used to refer to the mass movement of African-Americans from the South largely to the cities of the North, beginning in the early twentieth century but gathering pace after the First World War.

Harlem Renaissance Resurgence of African American artistic and cultural achievements based in the New York area of Harlem.

Hippies People who sought alternative lifestyles, often living in 'communes'. They often had long hair, flowing clothes and a liberal attitude to illicit drugs. They tended to resent authority and often came into conflict with the police.

Hobos Itinerant workers who wandered around the USA in search of employment.

Impeach Bringing a public official to trial over alleged wrongdoing in office.

Imperial power A country with an empire.

Imperial presidency Term to describe the growth in power of the presidency during the period 1961 to 1974.

Inflation Whereby prices rise and the value of money therefore falls.

Insider dealing Unfair practices on the stock exchange – for example, brokers getting together to fix prices.

Isolationism The policy by which the US involved itself as little as possible in foreign affairs.

Jim Crow Term given to segregation in the South.

Khmer Rouge Communist forces in Cambodia.

Korean War War 1950–53 to defend South Korea from communist North Korea.

Laissez-faire A policy of minimal government involvement in the economy.

Lend-Lease Wartime practice of 'lending' war materiel to the Allies, to be given back after the war.

Long drives Driving cattle from the ranches in the West to the nearest railhead for shipment east.

Lynching Illegal execution, usually by hanging, used particularly to terrorise African-Americans in the South and Mid-West.

Mid-term congressional elections Elections which take place every two years, halfway through the president's four-term period of office; usually a good indicator of the popularity of the president.

Miscegenation Historically used in a negative way to describe mixed racial relationships. More neutral terms like 'interracial' are used today.

Muckraking journalism Journalism of the progressive period which exposed scandals and social ills such as poor living conditions.

Napalm bombing Bombing settlements with a burning petroleum-based jelly called napalm.

Nationalisation of public utilities Where the state takes over the running of services such as electricity provision.

New Deal Name given to Roosevelt's programme to fight the Great Depression.

New immigration A term to refer to the immigration from southern and eastern Europe in the late nineteenth and early twentieth century.

New South The term given to the modernisation of the post-Civil-War South.

Oil crisis When sharp rises in the price of oil brought economic crisis to the West in 1973.

Patronage The means by which someone is given a position by someone who controls the right to do so.

President The head of state and chief executive of the USA. The president is elected every four years.

Primaries Method by which registered voters can vote for which candidate will represent the party in an election; some are closed, in which only recognised supporters of that party can vote, while others are open, in which all registered voters can vote irrespective of party.

Progressivism Early-twentieth-century movement to expand the role of government in dealing with social and economic problems and tackle corruption.

Pump-priming Expression used to suggest government spending would lead to economic growth.

Radical Republicans A group of Republicans who wished to punish the South after the Civil War and ensure the rights of African-Americans were protected in law.

Railheads The start of the railroad routes, to which cattle were driven in the West.

Reconstruction The period between 1865 and 1878 when the South was occupied by forces from the North and the process of its reintegration into the Union was undertaken.

Redeemers Those who sought an end to Reconstruction – they called this Redemption.

Republican Political party traditionally favouring business and less government intervention in the economy; supporters of *laissez-faire* policy but also the party which abolished slavery in 1863.

Rugged individualism Belief in people solving their own problems and not relying on the government for help.

Scalawags Southerners who collaborated with the new regimes during Reconstruction.

Seceding Breaking away from a state.

Second wave feminism The feminist movement of the 1960s: first wave feminism had focused early in the twentieth century on the fight to win the vote.

Secretary of State Presidential appointee responsible for foreign affairs.

Sharecroppers Farmers who rented land and were paid by the landowners a percentage of what they produced.

Skyscrapers Tall modern buildings in cities.

Space Race Rivalry between the USA and USSR to make the most progress in space exploration.

State Department US government department responsible for foreign affairs.

Subsistence Having just enough income to live on.

Supreme Court The highest judicial court of the USA, comprising nine chief justices whose main job is to check whether legislation is allowed under the constitution and whether practices at the different government levels are legal under the constitution.

Television evangelism Using television to spread the ideas of Christianity.

Urban renewal Term given to the regeneration of cities.

Utility companies Companies providing water, gas, electricity, etc.

Veterans' Association Ex-service people's associations.

Veto The ability to reject a proposed law.

Vietnamisation Policy associated with President Nixon of giving the South Vietnamese authorities more responsibility for fighting the war, with US aid.

Voluntarism The notion that business and state governments should solve the Depression through their own voluntary efforts.

War debts Debts accrued during the Great War, where the USA loaned the Allied powers the means to fight the war.

Watergate A political scandal in which evidence of the burglary and bugging of Democrat headquarters during the 1972 presidential election brought down the Nixon government.

'Yellow Dog' clauses Clauses which specified that, as part of their terms of employment, employees cannot join a trade union.

Yellow Press Term used to describe the sensationalist journalism in the 1890s.

Key figures

Andrew Carnegie (1835–1919) Carnegie is an example of the self-made industrialist who became a major philanthropist. He began his working life in a Pittsburgh cotton factory before moving into railroads. Profitable investments gave him a fortune which he used to begin steel production. In 1901 he sold his company to banker J.P. Morgan for $450 million, and thereafter devoted his life to philanthropy, building hospitals, libraries and universities for example. He is said to have given away over $350 million.

Grover Cleveland (1837–1908) Cleveland was a lawyer in Buffalo, New York. He entered politics as Mayor of Buffalo in 1881 and became Governor of New York. In 1884 he was elected president with a reputation for honesty and reform. He attempted some reform of big business practices during his period in office but with only limited success. He was the only president to serve two separate terms – in 1884–88 and 1892–96.

Dwight D. Eisenhower (1890–1969) A career soldier who became Supreme Allied commander in Europe during the Second World War, masterminding the invasion of Northern Europe in 1944. He became Republican president in 1953, and presided over 1950s prosperity and the developing 'arms race'. Eisenhower retained great popularity, although he was a conservative who was reluctant to move on issues such as Civil Rights.

Henry Ford (1863–1947) Ford set up his company manufacturing motor vehicles in 1903 and pioneered techniques of mass production which significantly reduced the cost of his cars. He moved to a large factory at Dearborn, Michigan, in 1917 where he acted as a paternal employer so long as employees toed the line. His economic success diminished as rivals such as General Motors emerged offering more choice and more advanced technology in their vehicles. Ford increasingly adopted right-wing political views before his death.

Herbert Hoover (1874–1964) A former mining engineer and millionaire businessman who served as Secretary of Commerce during the 1920s and became Republican president in 1929. His administration was dominated by his efforts to end the Great Depression but after his electoral defeat in 1932 he became a widely respected elder statesman.

Andrew Johnson (1808–75) Johnson came from a humble background and trained as a tailor. He was largely self-taught. He entered politics as a Democrat, becoming Congressman from the frontier state of Tennessee in 1943 and state governor in 1853. In 1865 he succeeded to the presidency on the death of Lincoln. His presidency was problematical: as a Southerner he was not trusted by Northern interests and faced impeachment. He was defeated in the 1868 election.

Lyndon B. Johnson (1908–73) Johnson was a teacher from Texas who was a fervent supporter of the New Deal. Elected to Congress in 1937, he rose through the political ranks to become Kennedy's vice president. He inherited the presidency after the assassination of the latter, and asked that Civil Rights legislation be passed as a legacy for Kennedy. He also introduced the ambitious Great Society programme but his presidency got bogged down in the Vietnam War and in 1968 he decided not to seek re-election.

John F. Kennedy (1917–63) Kennedy was born into a fiercely ambitious Irish-American family. A war hero in the Second World War, he entered Congress in 1947 and became Senator for his home state, Massachusetts, in 1952. In 1960 Kennedy was elected president. Although he won acclaim for his foreign policy, notably his handling of the Cuban Missile Crisis, much of his domestic programme was stymied due to opposition from a hostile Congress. He was assassinated in November 1963.

Martin Luther King Jr (1929–68) King was a Baptist minister and hugely influential Civil Rights campaigner. He first came into prominence during the 1955 Montgomery Bus Boycott, and later went on to lead many campaigns. He enjoyed wide national and international acclaim, winning the Nobel Peace Prize in 1964. King advocated peaceful protest. However, by the time of his death he was losing some influence in the face of more militant campaigners. King was assassinated in April 1968.

Huey Long (1893–1935) A popular politician from Louisiana who adopted the 'Share Our Wealth' programme. He was considered a viable rival to Roosevelt for the 1936 Democratic nomination for president before being assassinated.

Joseph McCarthy (1908–57) McCarthy was born in Wisconsin, trained as a lawyer and served in the US Marines during the Second World War: he was subsequently found to have exaggerated his war record. He became Senator in 1946 and achieved notoriety in 1950 when he initiated a communist witch-hunt with allegations of communist infiltration into government organisations. However, in 1954, McCarthy was censored by the Senate for his bullying tactics. He died of hepatitis worsened by alcohol abuse in May 1957.

Alfred Mahan (1840–1914) Mahan was a career naval officer who developed theories on the importance of naval power in making countries strong. His 1890 work *The Importance of Sea Power in History* was especially influential in the expansion not only of the US navy but others, for example the German navy. Mahan went on to write about other naval heroes such as Lord Nelson before his death in 1914.

William McKinley (1843–1901) McKinley was a teacher who became a Civil War hero. He entered Congress in 1868 and built up a reputation as a tariff expert, responsible for the 1890 tariff which bore his name. In 1890 McKinley became governor of his home state, Ohio. In 1896, after a fiercely fought election, he became president. His term in office was largely associated with the growth of US imperialism. In 1901 McKinley was assassinated.

Richard Nixon (1913–94) Nixon was a lawyer from California who was elected to Congress as a Republican; in 1950 he became a Senator, who supported McCarthy during the communist witch-hunts. He became vice president during the Eisenhower era, and was elected president in 1968. His presidency saw the development of détente, but was fatally marred by the Watergate scandal. Nixon was controversially pardoned for his part in the scandal and spent his latter years as a widely respected world statesman.

Eleanor Roosevelt (1884–1962) She was very active as First Lady, promoting in particular gender and issues of race. Eleanor often reported directly to her husband about whether New Deal initiatives were working. She was also a high-profile journalist who encouraged people to contact her with their concerns. She expanded the role of First Lady into a more active, political role.

Franklin Delano Roosevelt (1882–1945) Former Secretary of the Navy and Governor of New York, Roosevelt became president in 1932 at the height of the Depression. In 1924 he had contracted polio. His New Deal did much to transform the USA but enjoyed only limited economic success. Roosevelt remained president throughout the Second World War and died in office in April 1945.

Theodore R. Roosevelt (1858–1919) Roosevelt was born into a wealthy family, became interested in Republican politics and was elected to the New York State Assembly in 1881 as its youngest ever member. He grew fascinated by the West and spent time as a cattle rancher and deputy sheriff. He wrote best-selling books based on his experiences. On his return to New York, Roosevelt became Police Commissioner. During the Spanish–American–Cuban War he led a cavalry detachment known as the 'Rough Riders'. Roosevelt was McKinley's vice president so succeeded to the presidency after the latter's assassination in 1901. His presidency was noted for its progressive policies and imperialism. He was disappointed with his successor, Taft, and fought against him in the 1912 presidential campaign as an independent. This split the Republican vote and allowed Wilson to win.

William H. Seward (1801–72) Seward was a lawyer who became Governor of New York State from 1838 to 1842. He went on to become New York Senator from 1849 to 1861 when Lincoln appointed him Secretary of State, a post he held until 1869. During the Civil War perhaps his greatest achievement was keeping Britain out of the conflict. He was injured in the attacks which included the assassination of Lincoln in April 1865. During the years 1865 to 1869 he was a more expansionist Secretary of State than his predecessors, purchasing Alaska from Russia for instance. He retired after the defeat of President Johnson.

Harry S. Truman (1884–1972) Democratic Senator from Missouri, and vice president from January 1945, who unexpectedly became president on the death of Roosevelt in April. Truman made the decision to drop atomic bombs on Japan. He subsequently presided over post-war prosperity and the development of the Cold War.

Woodrow Wilson (1856–1924) Wilson followed a career as an academic, writing the hugely influential 'Congressional Government' in 1885 and becoming president of Princeton University in 1902. He entered politics as a reforming Democratic Governor of New Jersey, and became the 28th president in 1912. He followed progressive policies, and tried to keep the USA neutral during the First World War. However, deteriorating relations led him to declare war on Germany in April 1917. Wilson tried to broker a lasting post-war peace settlement. His health broke down during an extensive but unsuccessful tour to sell it in the USA.

Timeline

1862	Homestead Act
1865	Assassination of Abraham Lincoln
1865–78	Period of Reconstruction
1866	First Civil Rights Act
1866	Ku Klux Klan formed in Tennessee
1867	Purchase of Alaska and acquisition of the Midway islands
1868	Burlingame treaty with China
1869	Completion of first trans-continental railroad
1870	Foundation of Standard Oil
1873	Break-up of Tweed Ring in New York
1875	Whiskey Ring scandal
1882	Chinese Exclusion Act
1885	Interstate Commerce Act
1889	First Pan-American Conference
1890	Silver Purchase Act (repealed 1896)
	Sherman Anti-Trust Act
	McKinley tariff
	US Census Bureau declared the frontier closed
	Formation of the People's Party ('the Populist Party')
1893	Turner's thesis on 'The Significance of the Frontier in American History'
1896	Plessy v. Ferguson Supreme Court ruling
1898–99	Spanish–American–Cuban War
1898	Annexation of Hawaii
1899	Introduction of 'open door' policy
	Annexation of the Philippines
1901	Foundation of US Steel
	Assassination of President McKinley
1903	Elkins Act
	US take responsibility for the building of the Panama Canal

1906	Hepburn Act
1909	Foundation of National Association for the Advancement of Coloured People (NAACP)
1913	Underwood tariff
1914	Calydon Anti-Trust Act
	Completion of Panama Canal
1916	Seventeenth Amendment – popular election of Senators
1917	US entry into the First World War
	Espionage Act
1918	Sedition Act
1919	Eighteenth Amendment – introduction of Prohibition
1920	Nineteenth Amendment – gave women the vote
	Palmer Raids
1921	Budget and Accounting Act
	Emergency Immigration Act
	Sheppard–Towner Act
1924	Johnson–Reed Immigration Act
1926	End of the Florida Land Boom
	Presidency of Herbert Hoover began
	Agricultural Marketing Act
1930	Smoot–Hawley tariff
1931	Moratorium on foreign debts
	National Credit Corporation set up
1932	Johnson Act
	Federal Home Loan Bank Act
	Reconstruction Finance Corporation set up
	Emergency Relief and Construction Act
	Bonus Army march on Washington
1933 March	Emergency Banking Relief Act
	Farm Credit Act
	Civilian Conservation Corps

Quick quizzes at www.hoddereducation.co.uk/myrevisionnotes

	May	Glass–Steagall Act
		Truth-in-Securities Act
		Agricultural Adjustment Act
		Tennessee Valley Authority
		Federal Emergency Relief Act
	June	National Industrial Recovery Act
		National Recovery Administration
		Public Works Administration
		Home Owners Refinancing Corporation
	November	Civil Works Administration
1935	April	Emergency Relief Appropriation Act
	May	Resettlement Administration
		Rural Electrification Administration formed
	25 May	Black Monday
	June	Revenue (Wealth Tax) Act
	July	National Labour Relations Act
	August	Public Utility Holding Company Act
		Social Security Act
		Banking Act
1936		Roosevelt's battle with the Supreme Court (Judiciary Reform Bill)
1937		'Roosevelt Recession'
1941		Lend-lease act
		US entry into Second World War
1943		Race riots in Detroit
1944		Selective Servicemen's Readjustment Act ('GI Bill of Rights')
1945		Death of Roosevelt
		End of the Second World War
1946		Employment Act
		Iron Curtain speech
		Anthracite coal strike
		Threat of national railroad strike

1947	Taft–Hartley Act
	Truman Doctrine or containment
1948	Marshall Aid
	Berlin Airlift began
1949	China became communist
	USSR exploded its first atomic bomb
1950–53	Korean War
1950	McCarthy's anti-communist 'witch-hunt' began
1954	Brown v. Board of Education of Topeka Supreme Court ruling
1955	Montgomery Bus Boycott
1957	Little Rock school desegregation crisis
	Highways Act
1962	Cuban Missile Crisis
1963	Partial Test Ban Treaty
1963	Assassination of President John F. Kennedy
1964	Economic Opportunities Act
	Civil Rights Act
	Gulf of Tonkin incident
1965	Selma march
	Voters Rights Act
1966	Formation of National Association of Women (NOW)
1968	Assassination of Dr Martin Luther King
	Tet Offensive
1970	US invasion of Cambodia
	Kent State shootings
1971	Nixon's visit to China
1972	SALT 1 signed
1972–74	Watergate scandal
1973	Oil crisis
1974	Resignation of President Nixon
1975	Helsinki Agreements

Answers

Page 9, Spot the mistake

This is a narrative answer which does not directly address the question. Some of the material is relevant – for example, the fact that Republicans dominated Congress and disagreed with the president's view – but it needs to be pointed to the question.

Page 11, Interpretation: Content or argument

Student 1 is merely paraphrasing the extract. Student 2 gives the arguments which suggest that, while on the whole federal government may have been weak, the Senate itself may have been effective.

Page 15, Summarise the arguments

While the completion of the trans-continental railroad made internal markets accessible on a national basis, it was equally important in terms of its symbolic impact. It enhanced the optimism which already existed that anything was possible in the USA. The success of the USA was enhanced by more successes. The trans-continental railroad was significant here as the greatest feat of engineering at that time.

Page 17, Analysing an interpretation

You could consider issues such as the growth in agricultural production, the technical advances to make land more productive to show the successes in agriculture; you might consider the rise of the Granger movement to try to overcome difficulties such as debt. If you disagree with the interpretation you might argue that Kansas might not be typical; you could cite the sharecroppers of the South and the more affluent agriculture of the North near to the urban markets to argue against generalising from one case.

Page 17, Eliminate irrelevance

Irrelevant sentences: By this date the Union Stockyards covered over a square mile and supplied 80 per cent of the meat consumed in the USA. Much of the meat came from the ranches of the West and was delivered by the growing railroad network – which created many jobs in both the meat and railroad industry and was another reason for the growth of Chicago. By the 1890s skyscrapers were built with as many as 25 storeys. In 1902, 66 were being constructed in Lower Manhattan alone.

Page 19, Spot the mistake

This paragraph is too unfocused. Some of the comments address the question but most do not. It should first have examined how far measures undertaken represented the interests of the wealthy and big business and how far it represented the interests of other groups in order to come to a judgement based on the question.

Page 23, RAG – rate the timeline

1866 Application of Monroe Doctrine to stop French involvement in Mexico

1867 Purchase of Alaska from Russia

1867 Acquisition of Midway islands

1868 Ulysses S. Grant became president

1868 Burlingame treaty with China

1869 Trans-continental railroad completed

1870 Congress refused to annex the Dominican Republic

1871 Settlement with Britain over issues remaining from Britain's support for the Confederacy

1882 Chinese Exclusion Act

1884 James Blaine advocated closer links with Latin America

Page 33, Summarise the arguments

Populism was supported by the Southern farmers who relied on cash crops which had been affected by a worldwide depression and those employed in silver production in the West. However, its attraction was not simply economic. At its best Populism could be used to support social reform and, at its worst, to push conspiracy theories; in this case, that big business was responsible for economic problems.

Page 41, Use own knowledge to support or contradict

The main argument is that, despite some evidence to the contrary, evidence of racial conflict is overwhelming. However, total segregation did not have to be the result.

A counter-argument might be that segregation was being introduced as soon as Reconstruction ended and lynchings and violence were deployed to exclude African-Americans from public life. There were no influential voices advocating racial mixing or inclusion of African-Americans. Influential Southern voices such as Booker T. Washington seemed to accept subjugation.

Page 43, RAG – rate the timeline

1823 Monroe Doctrine

1890 Publication of Alfred Mahan's The Impact of Sea Power in History

1896 William McKinley became president

1898 Spanish–American–Cuban war

1898 Annexation of Hawaii

1899 Paris Peace settlement

1899 Division of Samoa between USA and Germany

1899 Annexation of the Philippines

1899 Philippines rebellion

1900 Boxer rebellion in China

1901 Assassination of President McKinley

1903 US involvement in the construction of the Panama Canal

1906 Algericas Conference

1908 Presidency of William Howard Taft

1914 Panama Canal completed

Page 43, Eliminate irrelevance

Irrelevant sentences: There was considerable unrest in Hawaii in the 1890s as a result of the growing influence of US growers. The Yellow Press had talked up Spanish atrocities to garner public support for the war. Spain was easily defeated.

Page 47, Turning assertion into argument

The first answer is simply a description. The second is an argument justified with reasons.

Page 55, Summarise the arguments

Johnson is arguing that Hoover should have followed the advice of his Treasury Secretary and let the Depression run its course. Mellon argued that if economic problems were left alone they would sort themselves out. Unsound business would go bankrupt but the sound ones would continue. As unemployment grew, wages would fall as more employees chased fewer jobs. However, Hoover believed high wages would the key to economic prosperity because people could buy more. He

therefore told the Federal Reserve to issue more money into the economy – £300 million in October 1929.

Page 55, RAG – rate the factors

1928 Kellogg–Briand pact

1928 Hoover's electoral victory

1929 The Wall Street Crash

1929 to 1933 Unemployment grew by 3.14 per cent to 24.75 per cent

1930 Smoot–Hawley tariff

1931 Repudiation of war debts

1932 President's Emergency Relief Committee

1932 Federal Home Loan Bank Act

1932 Reconstruction Finance Corporation

1932 Emergency Relief and Reconstruction Act

1932 Hoover defeated in the presidential election

Page 59, Turning assertion into argument

The first answer is simply a series of assertions with little in support. The second is made up of arguments with reasons in support.

Page 63, Eliminate irrelevance

Irrelevant sentences: This resulted in growing opposition to Roosevelt's policies as shown by the mid-term congressional elections of 1938 which saw large gains for conservative Democrats and Republicans. Roosevelt had once said that everyone was against him but the electorate but this no longer seemed to be the case.

Unlike in the First World War, women were widely recruited to make up the shortages: 6.5 million women were in the workforce by 1944. Between 1941 and 1945 the USA produced 86,000 tanks, 290,000 aircraft and 15 million rifles.

Page 65, Use own knowledge to support or contradict

The main argument is that Prohibition was unenforceable because both federal and state governments lacked the resources to do so. However, a counter-argument might be that in many areas Prohibition did succeed because local populations supported it, having passed Prohibition laws in their states before the First World War, and agents worked tirelessly to enforce it as far as possible.

Page 69, RAG – rate the timeline

1920 Census showed more than 50 per cent of Americans lived in urban centres of 2500+ population

1921 Ku Klux Klan had 21,000 followers

1923 Calvin Coolidge became president

1924 Ku Klux Klan helped elect four state governors

1926 50,000 Ku Klux Klan members marched through Washington

1927 Marcus Garvey deported

1929 Ku Klux Klan membership fell to 20,000

1929 Wall Street Crash

Page 69, Summarise the arguments

The extract argues that the Klan didn't only attack African-Americans but anyone it considered having 'unAmerican attitudes', for example accepting a strict moral code of behaviour. The inference is that their hatred was maintained for a wide variety of groups and therefore they contributed significantly to social tensions in the USA during the 1920s.

Page 75, Use own knowledge to support and contradict

The extract suggests Truman wanted to implement an ambitious social programme against the wishes of Congress. However, his programme was overshadowed by industrial action as a result of cuts in wages through loss of overtime and rises in living costs. The coal strike in particular threatened post-war recovery. This could be supported by reference to the programme and the intensity of the strikes. The difference in attitudes between Truman and Congress could be shown by their differing responses to the Taft–Hartley Act of 1947.

A counter-argument might be that Congress should have been more proactive and supported Truman's reform programme. For example, employers were bound to reduce overtime as wartime demand for goods diminished. Possibly Congress should have continued with price controls to reduce the immediate impact of these, maintaining them until the situation became more normal. Congress could also have been more sympathetic to Truman's social programme.

Overall Truman seemed worried that Congress wanted to revert to the *laissez-faire* policies of the Republican administrations which followed the First World War. This was exemplified by the way he got rid of wartime price controls while doing nothing to ensure a smooth transition towards peacetime wage levels.

Page 75, RAG – rate the timeline

1945 Death of Roosevelt

1945 End of the Second World War

1946 Coal strike

1946 Threat of national railroad strike

1947 Taft–Hartley Act

1953 Presidency of Eisenhower

1953 Creation of Department of Health, Education and Welfare

1956 Highways Act

1959 Balanced budget

1960 End of Eisenhower's presidency

Page 83, Summarise the arguments

The extract shows the diversity about opinions on youth revolt – from the arguments that it comes from issues such as lack of parental control to those who applaud youth for seeking a better world. The author dates it specifically to the Port Huron Manifesto. This gives specific reasons for revolt.

Page 85, RAG – rate the timeline

1945 End of the Second World War

1947 Truman Doctrine

1948 Marshall Aid

1948/9 Berlin Airlift

1950 Beginnings of McCarthy witch-hunt

1950–53 Korean War

1953 Death of Stalin

1961 Building of the Berlin Wall

1962 Cuban Missile Crisis

1964 Fall of Khrushchev

1965 Escalation of the war in Vietnam

1971 Nixon's visit to China

1972 SALT 1 signed

1975 Helsinki Agreements

Page 87, Eliminate irrelevance

Irrelevant sentences: Here North Vietnamese torpedo boats were alleged to have fired on a US destroyer. Even when the USA had become involved in a coup against the unpopular South Vietnamese leader Diem in November 1963 most Americans were unaware of Vietnam.

Quick quizzes at www.hoddereducation.co.uk/myrevisionnotes